On Pain

On Pain

Ernst Jünger

Translated and Introduced by David C. Durst

With a Preface by Russell A. Berman

Telos Press Publishing
Candor, NY

Printed in the United States of America
18 17 16 15 14 13   3 4 5 6 7

Translated by permission from the German original, "Über den Schmerz," in Ernst Jünger, *Sämtliche Werke*, vol. 7, pp. 143–91, Stuttgart 1980; 2nd edition 2002. First published in 1934 as part of *Blätter und Steine* with Hanseatische Verlagsanstalt, Hamburg. Klett-Cotta © 1934, 1980 J. G. Cotta'sche Buchhandlung Nachfolger GmbH, Stuttgart

ISBN: 978-0-914386-40-7

Library of Congress Cataloging-in-Publication Data

Jünger, Ernst, 1895–1998.
 [Über den Schmerz. English]
 On pain / Ernst Jünger ; translated by David C. Durst.
   p. cm.
 Includes bibliographical references and index.
 ISBN 978-0-914386-40-7 (pbk. : alk. paper)
1. Pain. I. Title.
 BJ1409.J8613 2008
 306—dc22
                                  2008032925

Telos Press Publishing
PO Box 811
Candor, NY 13743

www.telospress.com

CONTENTS

Preface to the Telos Press Edition of Ernst Jünger's "On Pain"

Russell A. Berman

Ernst Jünger's "On Pain" belongs to the current of thought of the so-called "Conservative Revolution" in Germany during the 1920s and 1930s, a deeply pessimistic critique of the society and culture of the Weimar Republic and liberal modernity in general. Building on nineteenth-century precursors, especially Nietzsche, the conservative revolutionaries expressed adamant contempt for the "bourgeois values" of individualism and sentimentality and generally denigrated the legacy of the Enlightenment, while looking forward to the imminent establishment of a new order made of sterner stuff. Like Nietzsche, they claimed to diagnose the loss of values and a loss of quality in the decadence of modern life. Yet while Nietzsche countered this decline with the myth of the superman as an aristocratic alternative to democratic leveling, the conservative revolutionaries, and especially Jünger, tried to identify a new heroism emerging precisely out of the technological world of the new mass society. If conventional conservatives emphasized a return to the past or, at least, a program to preserve traditions against the eroding forces of progress, the conservative revolution argued that the fundamental transformations at work in contemporary society could lead to an outcome defined by organized power, discipline, and a will to violence. The outcome of progressive modernization would, paradoxically, not be the standard progressivist utopia of free and equal individuals but a regime of authority beyond question.

In the translator's introduction to this edition of "On Pain," David Durst provides an admirable and encompassing account of the text, its context, and its reception. Jünger's essay is a vital document of German thought in the wake of the collapse of Weimar democracy. Durst locates it in relation to the German intellectual-historical tradition and the complex responses to modernity. A stance of "heroic realism" was viewed as a symptom of an emerging new culture, which Durst traces through important milestones in Jünger's writing. "On Pain" is an indispensable historical document for anyone interested in the underlying political and cultural stakes in the crisis that brought Hitler to power.

Far from the propaganda of the era, Jünger's cultural criticism is complex, thoughtful, and often trenchant in ways that distinguish it emphatically from Nazi screeds. No wonder he quickly ran afoul of the Party, as Durst describes. While "On Pain" does put forward illiberal positions, in some ways it frankly resembles the Critical Theory of the Frankfurt School as it developed in the period and with which English-language readers may be more familiar. It is not that cultural criticism on the right and the left, the Conservative Revolution and the Frankfurt School, converged, but quite understandably they did confront similar problems and pose comparable questions. Intelligent observers described the same social transitions, albeit from distinct perspectives, but with enough similarities to warrant comparisons. Although conventional political thinking still tries to police a neat separation between left and right, we should not be afraid to explore the gray zone in between without leaping prematurely or unnecessarily to an unwarranted assertion of identity.

Jünger's rejection of sentimentalist optimism and his insistence on the centrality of pain—by which he means loss, suffering, and death as well as genuine physical pain—to the human condition is akin to the dark vision of Schopenhauerian pessimism that suffuses Max Horkheimer's thought. The blithe confidence in a collective "forward" that marked, and still marks, progressivism is no longer on the table. Whatever the consequences of the tragic sensibility—and there are various possible outcomes—it precludes the characteristic mentality of the historical optimist, best allegorized by the frozen smile of an emoticon: happy days aren't here again. Of course Jünger and Horkheimer draw incompatible conclusions: Jünger predicts a new social type emerging from the existential condition of pain, while Horkheimer takes a historical pessimism as grounds for a possible social criticism.

In addition to this similarity to the melancholy of Critical Theory, another point of contact involves the technological transformation of art. Jünger's comments on a new aesthetic sensibility, or rather the post-aesthetic sensibility of photography, bear an uncanny resemblance to Walter Benjamin's contemporaneous account, especially in his now canonical "Work of Art in the Age of Mechanical Reproduction." Jünger's "On Pain" deserves a similar dissemination as an account of the real cultural revolution of the 1930s: "Photography, then, is an expression of our peculiarly cruel way of seeing. Ultimately, it is a kind of evil eye, a type of magical possession" (40). The new medium elicits a new affect, undermining the cozy hermeneutic community of the literate public sphere, and initiates a reorganization of the relationship of the mass public to political institutions. Finally, one can even argue a *Doppelgänger* resemblance between Jünger and Theodor Adorno. Both tend to present a historical time-line that emphasizes a fundamental break between laissez-faire liberal and post-liberal, collectivist cultural formations; they both share a post-Weberian suspicion of bureaucracy; and they are both allergic to facile sentimentality. Perhaps most importantly, Adorno and

Jünger present uncannily similar treatments of the demise of subjectivity. Jünger describes how humans turn themselves into objects as technology; for Adorno, this objectification is at the crux of a history of alienation. Of course their evaluations of this development could not be further apart. Jünger embraces technological post-humanity as a welcome alternative to effete humanism, while for Adorno the degradation of individuality entails a damaged life, the scars of which preserve the memory of suffering.

As a period document, "On Pain" is powerful. It provides important evidence regarding the cultural mentality in the wake of the collapse of the Weimar Republic: it makes the strong case for revolution as conservative, rather than as emancipatory, and it ought to be read next to other revolutionary appeals, from Lenin's *State and Revolution* to Bertolt Brecht's *The Measures Taken*. As a corollary to other documents, including both those of the Frankfurt School on the left and those of Carl Schmitt on the right, it adds an important dimension to our intellectual-historical understanding of the age. However, this edition of "On Pain" is not undertaken primarily for antiquarian reasons. (An antiquarian collection of historical documents has never been on Telos Press's agenda.) Rather, this remarkable essay has an urgency precisely because elements of its argument shed light on our own cultural condition, three-quarters of a century after its original publication. It is that contemporary relevance of "On Pain" that is particularly fascinating and that surpasses its documentary value with regard to culture at the end of Weimar democracy.

Yet before proceeding to some of the specific connections to contemporary culture, it is worthwhile to dwell on the implicit scandal of the argument itself and the moves that are necessary to carve out a space to discuss Jünger and his essay, published in the first year of the Nazi revolution. Separating

Jünger and the other Conservative Revolutionaries from the Nazis in effect gains some breathing space and shields them from the opprobrium anyone would deservedly face for too great a proximity to the Hitler regime. This separation is certainly justified. The Nazis themselves eventually turned on Jünger (as they would similarly reject Heidegger after an initial honeymoon), even though Jünger, at the moment of "On Pain," evidently imagined that his own understanding of cultural transformation had something to do with the current events in Germany of 1934. In other words, we are looking at a deeply conservative thinker at a crucial moment in European history and in the orbit of a catastrophic political movement, who appeared to understand, or misunderstand, the new dictatorship in terms of his own distinct cultural theory, and we are also somewhat brazenly suggesting a potential validity to parts of his cultural insights. To ask whether elements of Jünger's account were right (even if his values were wrong, and even if he misjudged the political reality) is provocative, because it blurs distinctions hard-wired into standard understandings of the political landscape and breaks a taboo (which of course was long ago broken with regard to Heidegger and more recently with Schmitt). Can one learn from thinkers who were thoughtlessly sanguine in 1934?

The provocation gets worse, though, for in addition to positing the credibility of some of Jünger's claims, we are also challenging simplistic assumptions about the historical moment. National Socialism did not appear out of nothing, full-blown in January of 1933; it had developed for years through a slow gestation, which however implies the fuzziness of the borderline between Weimar and Hitler, between democracy and dictatorship. As much as Hitler's accession to power marked a caesura, it was also a continuity, which means that no neat separation between before and after is tenable. The same holds for dogmatic distinctions between left and right, since, as we have seen, there are plenty of points of comparison between the Frankfurt School and the Conservative Revolution. The Critical Theorists were not Communists (even if they were sometimes Marxists), but they can reasonably be described as part of a left-wing field of discourse; Jünger was not a Nazi, but it is indisputable that he belonged to the conservative camp. Long before Hannah Arendt, however, the hypothesis of a linear spectrum between Communism on the left and Nazism on the right, separated by an impassable barrier, was called into question and recognized as narrowly ideological: the two totalitarianisms of the early twentieth century had plenty in common with each other—perhaps more than each had with its own retinue of maverick thinkers, all of whom, from left and right, addressed shared questions, mixing important insights with the characteristic naïveté of intellectuals of whatever leanings. Hence, the scandal: Benjamin and Schmitt, Adorno and Jünger, not as questions of influence but in terms of shared problems—because those combinations of left and right demonstrate the unraveling of the moth-eaten security blanket that never the twain shall meet. That older ideological segregation can no longer be upheld, as if the Berlin Wall of thinking were still intact.

That account, however, is primarily historical. The bigger scandal is the suggestion of the continued validity, the actuality, of figures of Jünger's thought: he has something to say to us today. To suggest that his essayistic enthusiasm of 1934 retains pertinence in the first decade of the twenty-first century implies that parts of totalitarianism, or some underlying cultural tendencies of totalitarianism, are still with us, and this claim could quickly unsettle the complacent sense of normalcy in which we live, the sense of security that the nightmares of the 1930s and 1940s are far behind us. In fact, the Jünger of

"On Pain" would hardly have been surprised at such assertions of continuity. Like Adorno and (with a modest variation) Benjamin, he proposed a binary historiography in which the individualist era of laissez-faire liberalism was coming to a rapid and appropriate end, replaced by a post-individual regime of the "worker" and "mobilization." Adorno's parallel concept is the totally administered society. These are of course not the same constructs, but each represents the respective thinker's articulation of an alternative to the liberal insistence on the primacy of the autonomous individual. From within either of these accounts, the continuity of post-liberal formations, from 1934 to today, would not at all be surprising; on the contrary, this is precisely the historical narrative that each projects. The very least one can say is that both suffer from an excessive determinism and a refusal to focus on the complexity of historical transformation. (To be fair, both thinkers in the postwar period modified the linearity of their historical thinking to recognize the reality of liberal democracy as a non-revolutionary regime.) Surely from today's perspective it would be ridiculous not to proceed from a clear recognition that both totalitarian regimes came to deserved ends, in 1945 and 1989, and, even more importantly, liberal-democratic political systems subsequently emerged that have frequently served their citizenry very well and always better than did the revolutionary regimes. No cohort fared better under totalitarianism than in liberal democracy, not even party cadre.

Is there nonetheless a totalitarian trace in postwar democracy? Or rather: is postwar democracy thoroughly immune to totalitarian contamination? The claim that Jünger's description retains even partial viability today suggests that the post-totalitarian world, the democracies after Nazism and after Communism, have been less than fully successful in retrieving the legacy of nineteenth-century liberalism. To be

sure, that classical liberalism may function as a norm for political thought and jurisprudence, but it does not map directly
onto the operations of our political institutions or the civic
culture that subtends them. Ours is no longer the social world
of J. S. Mill, and—this is the hypothesis here—Jünger was able
to identify some deep-seated illiberal tendencies in modernity,
which came to the fore in the experience of the totalitarian
movements and regimes but which, stripped of the historical
trappings of the Nazi era, continue to operate in contemporary culture. We may be invoking liberalism and its categories
of autonomy and individual freedoms, even as their viability
erodes.

This tension between liberal norms and illiberal lives should
be evident to any reader of "On Pain." As much as the essay
can be viewed historically as a record of the crisis atmosphere
in the first year of Nazi Germany, its important contribution
today is its highlighting of currents in historical totalitarianism that are uncomfortably, indeed painfully close to our own
society and culture. This is troubling, to say the least, and it
is therefore important to be clear and cautious. It would be
egregiously inappropriate to describe contemporary western
democracies as "fascist" or "totalitarian" or "Communist." (Or
it would be merely polemical, as when left extremists designate
the United States as fascist or equate it with Nazi Germany.)
The differences are enormous: our political cultures do very
well without the charismatic leaders or the paramilitary violence of "classical" totalitarianism, and even at times of war,
none of the western democracies engages in the systematic
mass killings that defined Nazism and Communism. Democracies are better than the totalitarian regimes, and we ought
to be able to articulate the grounds for this claim clearly and
insistently in the current war of ideas. Yet appropriate pride in
this difference should not blind us to underlying tendencies in

our culture, a dark side to an ongoing and dynamic modernization, that threaten the categories of liberalism and generate
a totalitarian temptation today. "On Pain" sheds a sudden light
on how close that radical alternative to bourgeois normalcy
remains. In this sense, Jünger's essay contributes to a critical
theory of the present. A few examples can demonstrate its
relevance.

To the extent that "On Pain" presents Jünger's particular
description of the transition from a liberal to a totalitarian
culture, it could seem as distant to us today as does that era
of Stalinism and Communism, part of a very different century. However, reading Jünger should caution us against
feeling too comfortable in our enlightened present, as if we
were safely separate from that violent past. Component parts
of that totalitarian illiberalism still litter our landscape like
roadside bombs. The cruelties of blood and soil still haunt us,
the killing fields of ethnic cleansing still thrive: 1934 is closer
than we would prefer to imagine, and this is nowhere more
evident than in the violence of jihadist terrorism. The defin-
ing war of our time derives directly from the milieu of "On
Pain." The specific connection between Nazism and Islamism,
i.e., between a classic totalitarianism and one of its offspring,
has been well documented and analyzed by Matthias Küntzel,
in his *Jihad and Jew-Hatred*, in which he describes how the
exterminationist antisemitism of Nazism came to define the
Islamist movement and its contemporary agenda: this is the
continuity thesis between the Conservative Revolution and
today.

Yet "On Pain" is not antisemitic. Perhaps one might make
the argument that in an account of Nazi Germany, which is
surely one way to read Jünger's text, avoiding a discussion of
racial policies in effect constituted an endorsement, but that is
a different sort of claim, resting on a sin of omission. However,

the salient connection between "On Pain" and jihadism is not about Jews: it is about death. "On Pain" celebrates violence and warfare. It sets killing as its goal, and even more than killing an enemy, any enemy, the ultimate goal is killing oneself, a will to self-sacrifice embedded in the machinery of warfare, while invoking subordination to some higher idea. Nor is such self-sacrifice even a great sacrifice. On the contrary, self-sacrifice is a credible option because one accepts how one's own life is of at best negligible value. Anticipating figures of thought from Schmitt's postwar *Theory of the Partisan*, Jünger provides the prehistory of the suicide bomber in this spirit:

> Recently, a story circulated in the newspapers about a new torpedo that the Japanese navy is apparently developing. This weapon has an astounding feature. It is no longer guided mechanically but by a human device—to be precise, by a human being at the helm, who is locked into a tiny compartment and regarded as a technical component of the torpedo as well as its actual intelligence. (18)

This is hardly the model of the heroic warrior who, in passion or rage, in defense of crown or virtue, willingly faces death. Instead Jünger describes the reduction of the personality through a thorough instrumentalization, a transformation of the formerly heroic warrior into a merely technical component in a way that dooms the soldier to a living death. The fighter willingly gives up life in the act of destruction not because of some extrinsic grievance nor driven by some passionately held ethical commitment but because of a total submission to authority. The regime of technology does not burgeon into a modernist utopia of mastery over the natural world but, instead, turns everyone into a cog in the machine. Communism's prediction that "all that is solid melts into air" seems foolishly optimistic when measured against the universal mechanization announced by Jünger. The preponderance of

technological organization goes hand in hand with a reaction-
ary sense of unquestioning obedience to the powers-that-be,
whatever they are. Ideology is at best a flimsy pretext, devoid
of substantive content. It is never the motivating force; that
would indeed be a too idealistic account, as if ideas mattered
more than deeds. Yet in the end, this celebration of life-denying
violence is nothing if not a script for one of the paradigmatic
actors of our age, the suicide bomber, including the terrorists
of 9/11.

This linkage between the cultural criticism of "On Pain"
and the attack on the World Trade Center is not mere speculation. Jünger proceeds to explain how the model of the Japanese
submarine with the instrumentalized soldier could easily be
extended to allow for suicidal aerial attacks: "Manned planes
can…be constructed as airborne torpedoes, which from great
heights can dive down to strike with lethal accuracy the nerve
centers of enemy resistance. The result is a breed of men that
can be sent off to war as cannon fodder" (18). Cannon fodder:
this is the way that the Nazis and the Communists waged war,
sending off masses of soldiers to their sure death. This is also
the way that revolutionary Iran fought Iraq, by sending hordes
of children, armed only with the plastic key that would open
the gates of heaven, to clear minefields. Jünger's insistence on
the centrality of pain as the driver of culture is cut from the
same cloth as the terrorists' documented affinity for death:
"You love life and we love death," said the al-Qaeda spokes-
man on a tape released three days after the Madrid bombing
of March 11, 2004, proposing a distinction between a warrior
movement of soldiers prepared to die and a complacent con-
sumerist culture. This is nothing if not a reprise of the early
twentieth-century German conservative contrast between
Händler and *Helden*, between British merchants and Prussian
heroes, that informed the Conservative Revolution. A soldier's

death-defying bravery may be admirably virtuous, but the death-embracing terrorists who are engaged in a war against our way of life exercise a perversely seductive attraction on parts of today's public, especially the intellectual fellow travelers of jihadism. "On Pain" helps us understand why.

Suicide bombers are symptomatic indications of the declining value of individual life: the lives of the innocent and arbitrary victims as well as the life of the bomber. These are not what might have been called "suicide missions" in earlier warfare: extremely dangerous undertakings from which escape was unlikely but not unthinkable. In contrast, in the new paradigm, the death of the subject is constitutive of the mission. Or rather: the goal of the mission is the death of the subject. Tellingly, suicide bombing as a technique has not met the condemnation of world opinion. Of course, each single attack may elicit responses deploring the violence, but there has yet to be a blanket condemnation, and certainly no prohibition of suicide bombing comparable to the international bans on certain types of weaponry. Gas warfare, chemical weaponry, cluster bombs, and land mines may all be prohibited, but not suicide bombing, betraying a deep-seated affinity for its inherent message of the death of the subject. For Jünger in "On Pain," this topic flies under the flag of the end of sentimentalism: reality demands that we arm ourselves against it, that we steel ourselves, harden our resolve, and renounce the juvenility of subjective authenticity. This is the point where the Conservative Revolution of the 1930s anticipates the anti-humanism of postwar existentialism, which eventually made its way into the universities in the guise of post-structuralism and, for example, Foucault's celebration of the "end of man." If postmodernism meant anything, it certainly involved the hypothesis that modernity had come to an end, and with it the various agenda of humanism, liberalism, and individualism.

This epochal claim, that the era of modernity had finished, was structurally congruent with Jünger's claims in "On Pain," only fifty years later and, as appropriate for the 1980s, without the implicit collectivism that pervades the 1934 essay. One might say that the Conservative Revolution surpassed individualism through an integration into a greater whole, while postmodernism tended to subvert individualism by undermining the coherence of the subject. This difference is hardly insignificant, but it puts both positions at odds with the paradigm of individual autonomy and liberal rights. When "On Pain" talks about the obsolescence of individualism and sentiment, it reminds us of the pervasiveness of a homologous discourse at the core of the postmodern humanities today. This is Jünger's actuality.

In fact, Jünger himself commented on the impact of the tectonic shifts in culture on education, and the gradual demise of liberal education, a process that continues around us today:

> A second zone of sensitivity is devastated by the assault on liberal education. The effects of this assault are much less apparent. This has various reasons, but the most important one is that we continue to idolize ideas that artificially support the principles of liberal education, especially the idea of culture. Yet this changes nothing on the ground, because the assault on individual liberty inevitably involves an assault on liberal education. (20)

Needless to add, Jünger endorses these assaults: for him, liberal education, culture, and liberty are all *dix-neuvième*, detritus of a former age. For us, however, Jünger is of interest not because of this endorsement but because of the connection he draws and its pertinence to contemporary higher education. In fact the number of students with access to liberal education, as opposed to vocational or pre-professional training, is small, and this erosion of "culture" carries with it, so Jünger suggests, an erosion of freedom. His point, however, is that the future lies precisely with that focused and disciplined order of training rather than with the liberal ideal of free inquiry:

> We can assume that in the future this new assessment of the value of free inquiry as the pillar of liberal education will correspond to a comprehensive transformation in the organization of educational practices as a whole. We are now in an experimental stage. Nevertheless, we can predict with some certainty that education will become more limited and more focused, as can be observed wherever the training of man as a type rather than as an individual takes precedence. (21)

Certainly contemporary shifts in higher education are not centrally mandated by the state (as Jünger tended to suggest). Without however fully discounting the role of government intrusion in education, one can identify immanent processes within universities that correspond to Jünger's account: the decline of the humanities, most obviously, and more broadly a tendency toward narrow specialization, just beneath the surface of interdisciplinarity. Whatever its benefits, interdisciplinarity can too frequently end up encouraging postmodern forms of eccentricity, idiosyncratic combinations defined by lateral moves rather than by some depth of disciplinary field. This networked knowledge tends to have a niche character and systematically avoids opportunities to dig down into the knowledge base of the interpretive communities of disciplines. It can dodge hard questions by running to other fields.

Jünger draws a connection, therefore, between the dismantling of humanistic education and free inquiry, on the one hand, and the emergence of specialized knowledge and established hierarchy, on the other. The immanent principle of the liberal arts was the autonomy of the individual personality and therefore just as involved in a trajectory of freedom as were the scholarly agenda of unencumbered research and academic freedom. It is this worldview of liberty that may be crumbling around us. The pedagogy of "western culture" that prevailed in American higher education in the half century after the end of the First World War—until 1968—certainly had its parochial limits, but its core content was emancipation: the triumph of democracy. This account has been pushed aside by a combination of philosophical anti-humanism (Heidegger's legacy reshaped in deconstruction), a cult of power (the post-structuralism of Foucault), scholarly specialization (an inability to present grand narratives), and some genuine expansion of interest in the world outside the West, due to the context of globalization. The legitimate curiosity about other cultures stands in an uneasy relationship to the theoretical frameworks. It is, after all, difficult to elaborate narratives of decolonization without the category of liberty, while in addition politically correct hesitations typically prevent critics from measuring post-colonial or anti-imperial movements and states with the metrics of liberal freedom. Yet every refusal to speak out against repression anywhere undermines liberty everywhere. The apologies that are regularly pronounced for post-colonial excesses undermine the credibility of governance as such. The point is that the culture of education once provided robust support for individualism and democracy. Today, that humanistic mantle has grown threadbare, and in its place one finds a decentered university in which pre-professionalism, arbitrary narrowness, and blunt ideology cohabitate, only dimly aware of each other and with no reason to aspire to a coherent epistemology that might question this sorry state of affairs. In the meantime, it has become the norm that the bulk of research is now externally defined through funding mechanisms, from industry, foundations, and government, while, especially objectionable, social class differences undermine educational access. Attending a poor high school may not preclude admission to college, but it probably means that the door is already closed to specific career paths that require higher levels of preparation. Jünger identified this process at an early stage:

> We observe, for instance, that in many countries certain fields of study are now closed off to the younger generations from social strata assigned a lower level of reliability. The existence of *numerus clausus*, as applied to individual professions, institutions of higher education, or universities, is also indicative of a determination to cut off education right from the start to specific social classes, such as the academic proletariat, based on national interest. Of course, these are just isolated symptoms, but they nevertheless suggest that the free choice of a profession is no longer an unquestioned social arrangement. (21–22)

In the eleventh section of "On Pain," Jünger turns to a final theme, a "colder order that bestows its unique character on our time of change" (31). Humanity grows distant to itself, it transforms itself into its own object, and it eliminates its subjectivity, replacing sentiment with organization and efficiency. If the original human use of tools initially contributed to the definition of the species, humanity has reached a stage in which it itself is only instrumental. "The growing objectification of our life appears most distinctly in technology, this great mirror, which is sealed off in a unique way from the grip of pain. *Technology is our uniform*" (31). It is important to remember that, unlike the many contemporary critics of technology, Jünger embraces this transformation of culture: uniformity eliminates the inefficiency of exceptions and imposes a disciplined and heroic order. Yet few critics of technology are as severe as Jünger in his estimation of the scope of cultural change, nor have they been as prescient in anticipating the transformation of life forms.

Jünger's central thesis is that objectification through technology replaces warm solidarity—or at least the bourgeois
pretense of authentic warmth—with cold organization.
The two parts of that result have to be addressed separately.
Organization: like many other thinkers, Jünger regarded the
emergence of the hypertrophic state, the expansive government of bureaucratic administration, as ushering in a new era
of rational control and bringing to a conclusion the liberal age
of separated powers. Today, after the collapse of Communism
and, more importantly, after the rollback of classical wel-
fare-state structures beginning in the 1980s, one can wonder
whether that enthusiasm for the big state just represents the
mentality of a distant historical moment. Such an argument
would posit further dismantling of the state, or at least the
centralized nation-states, and an expansion of alternatives:
federalist decentering, market principles (this is the neo-lib-
eral version), or regional administration, such as the European
Union. Yet, the jury is still out on the prospects for the smaller
state. In recent years, there have been repeated calls for a reen-
gagement of the state and an expansion of its mission: in the
wake of Hurricane Katrina, in the administration of education, and in the face of the current economic crises, especially
in the housing market. It may yet turn out that, in the long
run, the efforts to roll back government bureaucracy that
began with the "Reagan Revolution" constituted only a brief
episode in the ongoing history of state expansion—in which
case Jünger's account of the comprehensive organization of
society will be proven accurate.

However, it is the second part of his claim that is more
interesting: coldness. Communications technologies undermine face-to-face encounters while eliminating the separation
of public and private spheres, let alone any notion of a forty-
hour work week: email and cell-phone technology make us

perpetually accessible, and the domestic space is no longer a cozy refuge. New forms of digital "writing" simplify spelling and privilege monosyllabic and paratactic language; irony and subtlety, artifacts of another culture, do not carry well in electronic media. Given current interest in visual (as opposed to verbal) culture, Jünger's focus on photography is especially fascinating. Benjamin regarded photography and cinema as advances in rationality that could elicit critical recipients. Jünger looks at the same material and modifies the conclusion. If the result is rationality, it is cold rationality, in the spirit of de Sade:

> The photograph stands outside of the zone of sensitivity. It has a telescopic quality; one can tell that the event photographed is seen by an insensitive and invulnerable eye. It records the bullet in mid-flight just as easily as it captures a man at the moment an explosion tears him apart. This is our own peculiar way of seeing….Photography, then, is an expression of our peculiarly cruel way of seeing. (39–40)

Tracing that cruelty through the contemporary landscape would involve linking multiple phenomena, from the proliferation of ever more violent entertainment films through the self-mutilation required to distort one's life into the prescribed categories of social networking websites. The viewing public—in contrast to Kant's older literate and reasoning public—proves itself again and again drawn obsessively to catastrophic images. The repeated displays of the Twin Towers in flames responded to an instinctual need, far beyond any journalistic necessity. There is some subterranean affinity between the terrorist production of violence and society's addiction to violent images: no perpetual peace here. This frame sheds light as well on Abu Ghraib: not the mistreatment of the prisoners, which was certainly reprehensible although surely exceptional, but the compulsion to photograph that cruelty and then, afterward, the insatiable desire for the perpetual display of the cruel images. That their dissemination only compounded the degradation of the victims never limited their circulation; on the contrary, it probably only enhanced the pleasure of the gaze. The categorically liberal outrage at the rights abuse and inhuman mistreatment at Abu Ghraib coexisted comfortably with, indeed may have only been a pretext for, an uninterrupted viewing of pain. The whole world is watching, luridly.

Jünger also anticipates the way technology has transformed the body. Humanism proceeded on the assumption of the integrity of the human body, from Leonardo's anatomical sketches to the opposition to the death penalty. Yet advances in bioengineering undermine inherited assumptions:

> We are not only the first living creatures to work with artificial limbs; through the use of artificial sense organs, we also find ourselves in the process of erecting unusual realms with a high degree of accord between man and machine. This is closely connected with the objectification of our view of life and thus also with our relation to pain. (38)

If humanism still survives, it is only with the help of prosthetic appendages. Instead of reducing healthcare costs, new technologies take over greater parts of our lives. What was once the privileged home of authenticity, the realm of emotions, is now a matter of pharmaceutical management, just as the end of life has become a question of technics. Jünger's speculation on the intrusive expansion of technology into the realm of the body clearly anticipates the extensive recent discussions of the blurring between humans and machines. This is an unexpected leap, from the Conservative Revolution to cyborgs, but what they share is the dismantling of liberal humanism.

"On Pain" is uncannily contemporary. As embedded as it is in the specific situation of Germany in 1934, it identifies and analyzes with exceptional insight fundamental tendencies that define our society at the beginning of the twenty-first century. Liberal humanism is still under siege. Jünger applauded its demise, looking forward to a new order, which soon turned into an epochal catastrophe. Whether we can avoid a similar catastrophe is the question of our age. In order to defend the emancipatory content, the prospect of a free humanity, for the end of which Jünger clamored, a study of "On Pain" is indispensable.

TRANSLATOR'S INTRODUCTION

> Tell me your relation to pain, and I will tell you who you are!
> Ernst Jünger, "On Pain"

1.

Ernst Jünger (1895–1998) is widely regarded as one of the most important, if also most controversial, German writers of the twentieth century. A highly decorated World War I veteran, Jünger remains perhaps best known for the gripping memoir of his experiences as a shock troop commander on the Western front in *Storm of Steel* (1920), as well as his oblique critique of the Nazi regime in the acclaimed novel *On the Marble Cliffs*, from 1939.

Yet since the republication of his political writings from the Weimar Republic in *Politische Publizistik 1919–1933* in 2001, renewed attention has been given to Jünger the political essayist.[1] As a prominent intellectual in the right-wing nationalist circle of "Conservative Revolutionaries," Jünger was an outspoken opponent of Germany's first and fateful experiment with parliamentary democracy. In 1925, he notoriously stated that he "hated democracy like the plague" and advocated in its place an extreme, authoritarian, and militaristic nationalism. His writings of the 1920s and early 1930s capture the radical Right's criticism of liberalism as the worldview of the bourgeoisie and herald the rise of a new iron order across Europe

---

1. Ernst Jünger, *Politische Publizistik 1919–1933*, ed. Sven Olaf Berggötz (Stuttgart: Klett-Cotta Verlag, 2001).

based on authority, discipline, and sacrifice. This is no less true for his essay "On Pain" (*Über den Schmerz*), which first appeared in 1934, one year after Hitler's rise to power.

According to Jünger's own testimony, "On Pain" is the third in a series of investigations on the dawning age of mobilization, which he began with the essays "Total Mobilization" (1930) and *The Worker: Mastery and Form* (1932).[2] In "Total Mobilization," Jünger describes the enormous process of mobilization, both technical and spiritual, underway in the establishment of large military-industrial states vying for power across the globe. This process marks an end to the "golden age of security" (Stefan Zweig) that defined bourgeois life in nineteenth-century Europe. The dynamics of large-scale technology and mass society demand collective responses, in which the individual was no longer of value in his own right but only in relation to the state. As Jünger writes, in this age the individual can be "sacrificed without a second thought." This "transformed world," as he would term it, became nowhere more visible than in the Great War, where the battles of *matériel*, i.e., of heavy armor and artillery, "played out in dimensions in which the fate of the individual disappeared."[3]

Jünger's second, longer essay, *The Worker*, turns attention to the *Gestalt* (literally, "form," "figure," or "shape") or new, post-individualistic type of human being, whose historic mission lies in embracing this process of mobilization by subordinating his freedom to the imperatives of the state. *The Worker* proclaims the end of the bourgeois individual, whose liberal values have become obsolete. In the mass industrial societies

2. Ernst Jünger, "Preface," in *Blätter und Steine* (Hamburg: Hanseatische Verlagsanstalt, 1934), pp. 12–13.

3. Ernst Jünger, *Sturm* (Stuttgart: Klett-Cotta Verlag, 1979), pp. 10–11. Jünger published the story *Sturm* in serialized form in the *Hannoverscher Kurier*, a conservative daily newspaper, in April 1923. All translations are mine unless otherwise indicated.

of the twentieth century, individual liberty, security, and pacifism are replaced by authority, discipline, and militarism; just
as the soldiers in the trenches of the Great War had become the
day-laborers of death, so too do the workers of the post–World
War I era assume the steely shape of soldiers. Here, one no longer speaks of individual rights or private life, but of duty and
service to the state. In a symbolically charged gesture, Jünger
predates the preface of *The Worker* to July 14, 1932; in the age
of total mobilization, the former Lieutenant in Prince Albrecht
of Prussia's Hanoverian Regiment believed, the authoritarian
spirit of Prussia would supersede the liberal spirit of 1789 as
the preeminent ideology of European states. The revolution
to come would be based on conservative principles from the
Right. "The ideal of individual freedom," he later writes in May
1933, "has become meaningless over against a spirit that sees
happiness in rigorous discipline and service for great deeds."[4]
     Completing this series of essays from the early 1930s, "On
Pain" announces a new metaphysics of pain. It no longer seeks
the measure of man in the liberal values of security, liberty,
and comfort but in the capacity to withstand pain and sacrifice oneself for a "higher" cause. Over the course of the past
century, Jünger notes, the "spirit" of man has grown "cold"
and "cruel"; life appears ever more clearly as a "will to power,
and nothing else." With the eclipse of liberal culture through
the progressive objectification and functionalization of life,
it is only those most hardened against pain who will prevail.
Although perhaps the least known of the three essays, Jünger
himself considered "On Pain" to stand alone as the "most
advanced among his works" at the time.[5] What Jünger later
in life said of *The Worker* is no less valid for this "trilogy" of

     4. Jünger, "Untergang oder neue Ordnung?" in *Politische Publizistik*,
pp. 648–49.
     5. Jünger, *Blätter und Steine*, p. 13.

essays as a whole: "the developments in Germany fit into its framework, but it was not especially tailored for it."[6]

2.

The biographer Thomas Nevin once remarked that Jünger's intellectual production "calls no philosophical system to attention."[7] This statement is no doubt also true for "On Pain," at least in part. Jünger's essay is unorthodox in its approach to the problem of pain, and the author draws intellectually on a remarkably eclectic group of thinkers and artists of the past, from Flavius Josephus, Daniel Defoe, and Mikhail Bakunin to Hieronymous Bosch, Breughel the Elder, and Lucas Cranach. Yet below the surface, Jünger's essay gives expression to salient features of conservative thought as it had crystallized in Germany after the Great War.

As is often noted, Jünger's worldview, style of thought, and perception were trained in youth on the battlefield. For the soldier turned writer, the clash of forces has method; it brings clarity to an otherwise confused and chaotic world. Accordingly, in his political writings of the interwar period Jünger "seeks not solutions, but conflicts," not a neutralization or reconciliation of antagonisms, but a Nietzschean intensification of the struggle.[8] Drawing on Carl Schmitt's ideas on the political, Jünger writes in *The Worker* that clarity comes

> not by blurring the antitheses but through the fact that they become more irreconcilable, and that every region, even the most removed, assumes a political character. . . . This means for each of us not the dissolution but intensification of the

6. Quoted in Paul Noack, *Ernst Jünger: Eine Biographie* (Berlin: Alexander Fest Verlag, 1998), p. 143.

7. Thomas R. Nevin, *Ernst Jünger and Germany: Into the Abyss, 1914–1945* (Durham, NC: Duke Univ. Press, 1994), p. 4.

8. Jünger, "Der heroische Realismus," in *Politische Publizistik*, p. 555.

conflict....A real force utilizes its excess power not to avoid
oppositions but to drive straight through them....This
excess is what on this side of the zone of conflict appears
as inner certainty and, after the measure of forces, as
domination.[9]

In "On Pain," this logic of confrontation aims its sights
at the bourgeoisie, the arch enemy of the German radical
Right. Jünger's essay, as so much of his work from the period,
is anti-bourgeois through and through. The deep and bitter
resentment that front-line soldiers felt against the home front
after the humiliating collapse of the War effort, surfaces in
Jünger's implacable attitude toward the bourgeoisie as a whole.
In 1929, as the Weimar Republic entered its final phase of crisis, Jünger—a self-proclaimed "true and unforgiving enemy of
the bourgeois"—spoke openly of the "pleasure the decay [of
the bourgeois] gives us."[10] Despite his cool distance to the Nazi
leadership, which had long courted him, Jünger must have
felt some satisfaction that his prognostications on the "self-
dissolution of the bourgeois world" proved to be correct in
Germany as Hitler took over power in late January of 1933.

In developments spanning from communist Russia to fascist Italy, Nazi Germany, and even Fordist United States, Jünger
thus saw the era of the bourgeoisie coming to an end; its values,
habits, and very way of life had become incommensurate with
the times. This was especially apparent in the confrontation
with pain. According to Jünger, the bourgeois individual typically dwells in a "zone of sensitivity," where "security," "ease,"
and "comfort"—and ultimately "the body" itself—become the
essential core of life. Here, one seeks to avoid pain at all cost.

---

9. Ernst Jünger, *Der Arbeiter: Herrschaft und Gestalt* (Stuttgart: Klett-
Cotta, 1982), p. 81.

10. Jünger, "'Nationalismus' und Nationalismus," in *Politische Publizistik,* p. 507.

During the liberal nineteenth century, advocates of the Enlightenment were of the belief that pain, both physical and psychological, was something that science and technology could marginalize or even banish from human life. In "On Pain," Jünger notes the innumerable human efforts undertaken to eliminate pain. Philosophers prescribed the abolition of torture and slavery, doctors discovered vaccinations and the benefits of narcosis, psychologists sought to liberate the individual from the inner sufferings of mental disease, and politicians introduced systems of public insurance and welfare for the old, young, and unemployed. In short, the enlightened spirit of the age brought forth an entire civilized world of prosperity and security.

Yet this liberal Enlightenment belief in ridding the world of pain through reason and science proved to be more a prejudice than a reality. It was not only that the overriding aim of this "security" society, of a social order dedicated to abolishing pain, produced a world of inferior values and, in the end, an existentially vacuous life of "complacency" and "comfort." "Boredom," Jünger notes, "is the dissolution of pain in time." What is more, modern mass society and technology demand not less but ever greater human sacrifice. The age has grown cruel. One need only look to the countless victims of accidents due to mass industrial production and modern transportation or the "bestial" attack on the unborn for proof. And in the sphere of politics, as World War I showed, belief in humanity and the pacification of conflicts between hostile nation-states turned out to be but a grand illusion. War, conflict, and sacrifice remain an ineluctable dimension of human life; if anything, they are now assuming an ever more ominous, planetary dimension.

Drawing on Graf Otto von Bismarck (1815–1898), "Iron Chancellor" of Germany in the late nineteenth century and idol of the German Right, Jünger thus concludes that "an essential conviction of all conservative thinking" is that "pain is among the unavoidable facts of the world." Pain, not pleasure; risk and sacrifice, not security; conflict, not comfort are axiomatic assumptions of conservative politics. A "noble detachment" from human suffering is thus requisite for conservative rule, for which there are more important things than pain.

This conviction of conservative thought concerning the ineluctability of pain strikes at the very foundations of the modern liberal state, upon which the first German democratic Republic was built. Beginning with Hobbes, the modern liberal state was no longer to be founded on aristocratic virtues, such as honor, pride, or duty, but instead on a new bourgeois worldview rooted in the individual right to self-preservation. For Hobbes, it was above all "vanity," the original, noxious source of aristocratic ideals, that constitutes the root cause of all evil. Vanity blinds man; by contrast, the diametrically opposed passion, fear, enlightens, and fear of violent death compels prudence. Not a belief in honor or valor in glorious deeds of sacrifice for the state, but the desire to pursue one's own private pleasures in peace and security forms the rational basis for the modern liberal state. An overriding goal of the modern liberal state thus rests in reducing the pain and suffering of its citizens. Duty to the state is no longer natural or absolute, but contingent upon the security that the state provides for private individuals to reap the fruits of peaceful coexistence in the arts, agriculture, and commerce. Hence, the *Leviathan*'s famous line: "The end of obedience is protection."[11] Yet based as it is on this novel set of bourgeois values, Hobbes's new political science cannot but progressively reject older aristocratic virtues, such as honor and pride, which are

11. Thomas Hobbes, *Leviathan* (Cambridge: Cambridge Univ. Press, 1996), p. 153.

inconsistent with fear, pain, and risk. This is especially the case with the virtue of courage, which, as Aristotle defines it in his *Nicomachean Ethics*, is concerned with

> the things that inspire fear; for he who is undisturbed in face of these and bears himself as he should towards these is more truly brave than the man who does so towards the things that inspire confidence. It is for facing what is painful, then, as has been said, that men are called brave. Hence also courage involves pain, and is justly praised; for it is harder to face what is painful than to abstain from what is pleasant.[12]

Jünger's conviction that the downfall of the bourgeois order is a consequence of this denial of courage was no doubt influenced in its articulation by his friend Carl Schmitt. In correspondence from the early 1930s, Jünger and Schmitt exchanged ideas on a range of topics related to their work, including not only Schmitt's concept of the political as "friend-enemy relation" but also Hobbes's ideas on fear and pain.[13] Jünger read Schmitt's *The Concept of the Political* and no doubt would have found in Schmitt's short but striking discussion of Hegel's "polemically political definition of the bourgeois" enormous resonance with his own ideas. In the passages added to the 1932 edition of *The Concept of the Political*, Schmitt writes that the young Hegel describes the bourgeois as

> an individual who does not want to leave the apolitical risk-less private sphere. He rests in the possession of his private property, and under the justification of his progressive individualism he acts as an individual against the totality.

12. Aristotle, *Nicomachean Ethics*, trans. W. D. Ross (Oxford: Clarendon Press, 1908), bk. 3, pt. 9.

13. See Jünger's letters to Carl Schmitt, dated December 13, 1933, and April 20, 1934, in *Ernst Jünger, Carl Schmitt: Briefe 1930–1983*, ed. Helmuth Kiesel (Stuttgart: Klett-Cotta, 1999), pp. 18–19, 24–25.

> He is a man who finds his compensation for his political
> nullity in the fruits of freedom and enrichment and above
> all "in the total *security* of its use." Consequently he wants
> to be spared courage [*Tapferkeit*] and exempted from the
> danger of violent death.[14]

But beyond Schmitt or even Hegel, we can trace Jünger's
view of the bourgeoisie in relation to the question of courage above all to Friedrich Nietzsche. Jünger read Nietzsche's
The Will to Power and *The Birth of Tragedy* a year before the
outbreak of the First World War, and, according to biographer
Heimo Schwilk, this experience had an "explosive" effect on
the eighteen-year-old. "Repulsed by the conventions of Wilhelmine Germany," Schwilk notes, "Jünger felt attracted to
Nietzsche and was enthralled by his devastating critique of the
bourgeoisie."[15] Indeed, it was none other than Nietzsche, an
intellectual shock trooper for the radical Right in Germany
especially after the Great War, who saw in the bourgeois individual's "sensitivity to pain," "inward acts of cowardice" and
"lack of courage," signs of the mediocrity, decay, and nihilism of European civilization as a whole.[16] What was this "Last
Man," of which Nietzsche so menacingly spoke, if not the individual who "loses courage and submits" when "faced with this
tremendous machinery" of nineteenth-century mass society?[17]
It was this same kind of cowardly figure that Jünger would
come across in Louis-Ferdinand Céline's *Journey to the End of
the Night*, which he read just as he was completing "On Pain"
in early 1934. In this celebrated semi-biographical novel from

14. Carl Schmitt, *The Concept of the Political*, exp. ed., trans. George
Schwab (Chicago: Univ. of Chicago Press, 2007), pp. 62–63.

15. Heimo Schwilk, *Ernst Jünger: Ein Jahrhundertleben: Die Biographie*
(Munich: Piper Verlag, 2007), p. 87.

16. Friedrich Nietzsche, *The Will to Power*, trans. Walter Kaufmann
(New York: Vintage, 1968), pp. 32, 167.

17. Ibid., p. 23.

1932, Céline, whom Jünger called the "Rabelais of a completely worthless world," depicts the nihilistic anti-hero Bardamu in his aimless flight from the trenches of World War I to colonial Africa, Fordist America, and the working-class slums of post-war Paris.[18]

Nietzsche's influence is not only present in Jünger's antipathy toward the bourgeois individual as the "Last Man," but also in the rediscovery of the virtue of manliness for the modern world. In *The Will to Power*, Nietzsche embraces the idea of a "new courage" with "no *a priori* truths…but a free subordination to a ruling idea that has its time."[19] This no doubt left its trace on Jünger. Already in his field notebooks during the War, the young soldier expresses his conviction that "courage is the only virtue of man."[20] And in *The Battle as Inner Experience* (1922), notorious for its lust for war and blood, Jünger writes:

> …courage is the wind that drives to far coasts, the key to all treasures, the hammer that crafts great empires, the armor without which no culture exists. Courage is the effort of one's own person to the last consequence, the jump start of an idea against matter, without care for what comes of it. Courage means to let oneself be nailed to the cross for one's cause. Courage means, in the last moment of life, to still show allegiance to the thought for which one stood and fell. To the devil with the times that want to take from us courage and men.[21]

Yet no one captures this Nietzschean pathos of courage as a kind of *amor fati*, a standing one's ground at a lost post or,

18. See Jünger's letter to Schmitt, dated January 2, 1934, in *Ernst Jünger, Carl Schmitt: Briefe 1930–1983*, p. 21.

19. Nietzsche, *The Will to Power*, p. 459.

20. Schwilk, *Ernst Jünger*, p. 122.

21. Ernst Jünger, *Der Kampf als inneres Erlebnis*, in *Werke*, vol. 7 (Stuttgart: Klett-Cotta, 1960), p. 52.

better, in a lost world, more strikingly than Jünger's intellectual mentor of sorts, Oswald Spengler. In the final section of *Man and Technics* (1931), Spengler writes:

> There is only one world-view that is worthy of us, and which has already been discussed as the Choice of Achilles—better a short life, full of deeds and glory, than a long life without substance. The danger is so great, for every individual, every class, every people, that to cherish any illusion whatsoever is deplorable. Time cannot be stopped; there is no possibility for prudent retreat or wise renunciation. Only dreamers believe there is a way out. Optimism is cowardice. We are born into this time and must courageously follow the path to the end as destiny demands. There is no other way. Our duty is to hold on to the lost post, without hope, without rescue, like the Roman soldier whose bones were found in front of a door in Pompeii, who, during the eruption of Vesuvius, died at his post because they forgot to relieve him. That is greatness.... The honorable end is the one thing that can not be taken from a man.[22]

This "heroic realism" or cult of courage and sacrifice was the German radical Right's response to a modern world in decline. In what Jünger himself calls "a last and most remarkable phase of nihilism," the only remaining virtue is courage, i.e., *andreia* or manliness, the original ideal of the heroic Greek world.[23] Yet in contrast to Nietzsche, for whom manliness remained a virtue of the wise and noble few, Jünger transforms this ideal by linking it with the will of the *Arbeiter*. In "On Pain," courage is transformed into the "discipline" and "detachment" of the worker; an essential, if no longer noble, capacity to hold

    22. Oswald Spengler, *Man and Technics: A Contribution to a Philosophy of Life* (Honolulu, HI: Univ. Press of the Pacific, 2002).
    23. See here Leo Strauss's account of Jünger's "On Pain" in Strauss's "Living Issues in German Postwar Philosophy," in Heinrich Meier, *Leo Strauss and the Theologico-Political Problem* (Cambridge: Cambridge Univ. Press, 2006), p. 128.

out in the "zone of pain." In the exacting age of total mobilization, the courageous warrior hero is replaced by the obedient
laborer of sacrifice and death. The worker no longer tries to
anesthetize pain but instead seeks to master pain and organize
life so that he is armed against it at every turn.

With remarkable perspicuity, Jünger anticipates here the
rise of a new breed of men who become one with new, terror-
izing machines of death and destruction. Equipped with an
unmatched ability to treat oneself in a cold and detached way
as an object, this worker-type makes possible human guided
"torpedoes" and "manned planes" that—like later the Kami-
kaze pilots of World War II—"can dive down to strike with
lethal accuracy the nerve centers of enemy resistance." Indeed,
Jünger's vision of manned missiles seems to reflect a logic that
later inspired the design of the Daimler Benz Project "F" in
Nazi Germany during the final years of World War II. The
DB "F"s were manned jet aircraft holding 3000 kg of explosives
that were to be launched from a long-range carrier aircraft
(the DB "C" or "Amerikabomber") once the enemy target was
in visual range. The pilot of the DB "F" was to eject through
an escape hatch located beneath the cockpit and parachute to
safety once he was assured of the hit. In reality, the mission
meant almost certain death for the pilot. According to Albert
Speer, with these manned missiles Hitler dreamed of turning
the skyscrapers of Manhattan into "huge burning torches."[24]

In "On Pain," Jünger also traces how this altered relation to
pain is inscribed in new patterns of human appearance, education, and organization emerging in the age of mobilization.
The physiognomy of the bourgeois, for instance, is "delicate,
pliant, changing, and open to the most diverse and distracting

---

24. Quoted in Matthias Küntzel, *Jihad and Jew-Hatred: Islamism, Nazism
and the Roots of 9/11*, trans. Colin Meade (New York: Telos Press Publishing,
2007), p. xix.

kinds of influences"; it reflects a life and culture of noncommittal ease, vacuous comfort, and security. By contrast, the face of the worker is "resolute and hardened through rigorous training; it possesses clear direction and is single-minded, objective, and unyielding." These latter are the steely, yet inwardly emptied-out, faces of Hitler's worker-soldiers, which Leni Riefenstahl would capture on film in *Triumph of the Will* (1935), parading with shovels in hand at the Nazi's Nuremberg Rally in 1934. Receiving rigorous, narrow, specialized training and taught to act no longer individually but as a unit, the worker is able to view himself dispassionately as an object ready for service and sacrifice for a "higher," collective cause. In a plain, unambiguous fashion, requiring neither moral deliberation nor doubt, the worker responds to all life's challenges as if obeying a command, i.e., beyond good and evil. Hence, the predilection for uniforms, masks, and sports. This differs dramatically from the *habitus* of the liberally educated bourgeoisie, which, as the dissolute and distracted masses, "are moved morally." As Jünger writes, "they unite in situations of excitement and indignation. They must be convinced that the opponent is evil and that they are prosecuting justice against this evil."

But the peculiarity of the worker is not only visible in outward physical appearance, training, or group dynamic; more importantly, it can be seen in the way that this new race of men views the world. According to Jünger, technology breeds discipline ("*Technology is our uniform*"), and this was nowhere more apparent than in photography. In a reversal of his earlier, negative opinion of photography, at the end of the 1920s Jünger became captivated by the possible uses of the photographic apparatus to advance the political cause. During the final years of the Weimar Republic, Jünger, his brother Friedrich Georg, and his friend Edmund Schultz collaborated on several fascinating, yet today little known, photo books, which covered topics ranging from the sorry state of parliamentary democracy in Germany to the rise of authoritarian worker-states on the ashes of the bourgeois world.[25] In all these efforts, as Jünger noted already in *The Worker*, photography should assume the role of "a political weapon of assault."[26]

The use of photography as a political weapon was by no means an invention or monopoly of the German Right. In the late 1920s and early 1930s, the newspaper publisher Willi Münzenberg (1889–1940) and his left-wing colleagues sought to form a cadre of worker-photographers who would regard "the photographic image as their weapon" and "the camera as a weapon in the struggle of the proletariat."[27] With the radical polarization of fronts during the last, intense years of the Republic, parties across the political spectrum ever increasingly chose the visual image over rational persuasion in their attempts to mobilize the masses. Photo magazines of all stripes sprouted up as vehicles for the dissemination of political views among the masses and proved to be an effective means in the mass struggle for political power. Here, one only

25. See here *Die veränderte Welt: Ein Bilderfibel unserer Zeit: 1918–1932*, ed. Edmund Schultz, intro. Ernst Jünger (Breslau: Korn Verlag, 1933); *Das Gesicht der Demokratie*, ed. Edmund Schultz, intro. Friedrich Georg Jünger (Leipzig: Breitkopf & Härtel, 1931).

26. Jünger, *Der Arbeiter*, p. 122.

27. John Heartfield, for instance, chose the motto "Benütze Foto als Waffe" ("Use Photo as a Weapon") for his display of works at the International *Werkbund* exhibition "Film and Photo" held in Stuttgart in 1929. See here Elisabeth Patzwall, "Zur Rekonstruktion des Heartfield-Raums der Werkbundausstellung von 1929," in Peter Pachnicke and Klaus Honnef, eds., *John Heartfield* (Cologne: Dumont Buchverlag, 1991), pp. 294–99; and John Willett, *Heartfield versus Hitler* (Paris: Éditions Hazan, 1997), p. 50. For a discussion of the function of the "Arbeiter-Fotograf" and the use of the "Foto als Waffe," see Edwin Hoernle, "Das Auge des Arbeiters," in Wolfgang Kemp, ed., *Theorie der Fotografie*, vol. 2, *1912–1945* (Munich: Schirmer/Mosel, 1984), pp. 224–27.

needs to think of John Heartfield's famous photomontages on the cover of the pro-Communist *Arbeiter Illustrierter Zeitung* or *AIZ* (*Worker's Illustrated Magazine*) and collected in Kurt Tucholsky's *Deutschland, Deutschland über Alles* (1929). With instantaneous clarity, one image conveys what a thousand words often could not achieve.[28]

Yet, for Jünger, the revolutionary nature of photography lies not only in the fact that "the appeal to immediate visual perception works more powerfully and incisively than the precision of concepts" in mobilizing the masses.[29] More fundamentally, the photographic apparatus is a "weapon of the worker" because it reflects what he calls the "second, colder consciousness" of the worker and his "peculiarly cruel way of seeing." In the War, Jünger recognized the decisive value of optical instruments that technically enhance the penetrating power of the human eye. Exposure to enemy reconnaissance or the scope of a rifle meant almost certain death. But the photographic apparatus too has a telescopic quality that stands outside the bourgeois "zone of sensitivity." As Jünger writes, "one can tell that the event photographed is seen by an insensitive and invulnerable eye. It records the bullet in mid-flight just as easily as it captures a man at the moment an explosion tears him apart." Through its objective lens, the camera is capable not only of "hunting down the individual" by exposing his hidden, private spheres of life, but also of destroying in a flash the substance of cultic worlds. "Ultimately," he writes, the photographic apparatus "is a kind of evil eye"; as such, it is akin to the worker, for whom "seeing is an act of assault." In short, the worker, like photography itself, captures the world in a cold, cruel, and colonizing way, beyond good and evil.

---

28. Kurt Tucholsky, *Deutschland, Deutschland über alles*, trans. Anne Halley (Amherst: Univ. of Massachusetts Press, 1972).

29. Ernst Jünger, "Einleitung," in *Die veränderte Welt*, p. 5.

Jünger's ideas on photography resonated with other, ongoing efforts in Germany at the time. In autumn of 1933, for
instance, the German Museum in Munich held the exhibition
Die Kamera, which was designed to mobilize professional and
amateur photography for the new tasks of National Socialism.[30] It follows a call of the Nazi journal *Photofreund* from
July 1933, in which the editors spoke out in favor of a "German photography" that would "no longer distract from the
struggle [of National Socialism]; no, photography should
lead into it, become an instrument, a weapon in the struggle.
And that photography can be a sharp and powerful weapon,
the men of the new Germany have recognized this with clear
vision."[31] As was often the case, Jünger acted as a kind of seis-
mograph of the times.

It causes us little wonder, then, when the inside caption of
the international editions of *Blätter und Steine* published in the
early 1940s would claim the following in eloquent English: "in
the war chapters and above all when dealing with the problem
of pain, Jünger sets forth a view of the world which typifies
and brings into sharp relief a whole generation of Germans."
Indeed, it is hard to deny just how true this was. For in snap-
shots that German soldiers took of their "adversaries" during
the first successful months of Operation Barbarossa in 1941,[32]

---

30. Hanno Loewy, "'…ohne Masken': Juden im Visier der 'Deutschen
Fotografie' 1933–1945," in Klaus Honnef et al., ed., *Deutsche Fotografie:
Macht eines Mediums 1870–1970* (Cologne: Dumont, 1997), p. 135. For a
discussion of *Die Kamera* exhibition of 1933, see also Ulrich Pohlmann,
"'Nicht beziehungslose Kunst, sondern politische Waffe': Fotoausstellungen
als Mittel der Ästhetisierung der Politik und Ökonomie im Nationalsozia-
lismus," in *Fotogeschichte: Beiträge zur Geschichte und Ästhetik der Fotografie*,
Jg. 8, Heft 28 (1988), pp. 17–32.

31. Quoted in Loewy, "'…ohne Masken,'" p. 135.

32. See here Daniel Goldhagen, *Hitler's Willing Executioners* (New York:
Random House, 1997), pp. 245f.; Loewy, "'…ohne Masken,'" pp. 135–49;
Dieter Reifarth and Viktoria Schmidt-Linsenhoff, "Die Kamera der Henker:

we find a most convincing illustration of what Jünger referred to as "our peculiarly cruel way of seeing." German soldiers not only perpetrated abominable crimes against humanity, but they also took photos of their victims in humiliating scenes and made these "trophies of war" available on order for the amusement of others. These heinous acts reveal a peculiarity of German fascism, a cold, cruel, and colonizing gaze that Jünger seems to have heralded.

All the more remarkable, then, is Jünger's own personal reaction to the atrocities of the Nazi regime perpetrated by German soldiers, SS, and Wehrmacht during the Second World War. Especially in his diaries, *Radiations (Strahlungen)*, Jünger's response to reports of the systematic murder of thousands of Jews by the SS while on duty in the Caucasus in the fall of 1943 and, later, to the sight of emaciated Jews just released from the Belsen concentration camp in 1945 is not of a man detached from suffering or sure of himself in the zone of pain and discipline. Shaken by the sight of Holocaust survivors, Jünger writes: "Only the sight of the individual, of the nearest, can reveal to us the suffering of the world."[33]

3.

Jünger wrote "On Pain" in the early months of 1934 while residing in the medieval town of Goslar am Harz, located in Lower Saxony.[34] Goslar, it should be noted, was the first station of Jünger's "internal emigration" during the Nazi period. In 1932,

Fotographische Selbstzeugnisse des Naziterrors in Osteuropa," in *Fotogeschichte: Beiträge zur Geschichte und Ästhetik der Fotografie*, Jg. 3, Heft 7 (1983), pp. 57–71; and Klaus Theweleit, *Männerphantasien 1+2* (Munich: Piper, 2000), pp. 493f.

33. Ernst Jünger, *Sämtliche Werke*, vol. 3, *Strahlungen II* (Stuttgart: Klett-Cotta, 1979) p. 425.

34. Helmuth Kiesel, *Ernst Jünger: Die Biographie* (Munich: Siedler, 2007), p. 435.

Jünger was threatened in the Nazi press with "Kopfschüsse," or "bullets to the head," because of the collectivistic tendencies in *The Worker*. And after his apartment in Steglitz was raided by the Nazis in April 1933, Jünger thought it wise to remove himself from Berlin altogether.

"On Pain" was the final essay in *Leaves and Stones* (*Blätter und Steine*), a collection of his shorter essays that appeared in print in the autumn of 1934. This essay collection bridges Jünger's passage from an author of earlier published war and mobilization texts from the Weimar period, such as "Fire and Movement" (1930) and "Total Mobilization" (1930), to an author of "internal emigration," as reflected in the "Epigrammatic Appendix." This appendix was a compilation of one hundred epigrams, several of which were a direct challenge to the Nazi regime.

The publisher of *Leaves and Stones* was the Hanseatische Verlagsanstalt (HAVA) in Hamburg. As the biographer Helmuth Kiesel states, collaboration with HAVA, which began in 1929 with *The Adventurous Heart*, was a stroke of luck for Jünger.[35] As publisher of *On the Marble Cliffs* (1939) and *The Peace* (1945), HAVA would back Jünger's stance toward the Nazis throughout Hitler's rule. Indeed, HAVA would become known as the "Verlag des 20. Juni" ("Publisher of the 20th of June, 1944"), i.e., the date of the failed plot to assassinate Hitler, for its support of voices, like Jünger's, critical of the Nazi dictatorship.

Like much of Jünger's work in Nazi Germany, *Leaves and Stones* fared well on the market. In the early 1940s, the collection of essays was republished three times and with only one minor footnoting change in "On Pain." After the Second World War, "On Pain" did not reappear in print until 1960, when it was published in *Essays I: Betrachtungen zur Zeit* (*Essays I:*

35. Ibid., pp. 436–37.

Observations of the Times), the fifth volume of Jünger's first edition of his complete works, *Werke*. Jünger made significant revisions to "On Pain" for this edition. These modifications included numerous stylistic changes as well as the addition and deletion of several passages. For example, Jünger removed a sentence in section 9 on the massacre of the intelligentsia during the Russian Revolution; and at the end of section 8, he added a short paragraph on a terrorist's readiness to blow himself up to avoid arrest in Joseph Conrad's novel *The Secret Agent* (1907). Of the changes made, however, few, if any, it seems were intended to render the text more palatable for a post–World War II audience, something Jünger had been criticized for by his former secretary Armin Mohler with respect to other works he had revised for republication. With only slight stylistic modifications, this 1960 version of "On Pain" was then taken up in *Essays I*, the seventh volume of his *Complete Works* (*Sämtliche Werke*) published in 1983. This final version is the text used for the current translation.

"On Pain" is a provocative text. Jünger's uncompromising criticism of bourgeois security, ease, and complacency might be best ascribed to what Thomas Nevin fittingly calls the "Protestant horror of comfort" found in many of his writings. And Helmuth Kiesel describes Jünger's positive embrace of pain and human sacrifice in "On Pain" as "unscrupulous and cold."[36] Indeed, "On Pain" charts a new, post-humanistic vision of man, which seems to reject the Pauline belief that, although "the whole creation groaneth and travaileth in pain together until now" (Romans 8:22), mankind will find salvation and deliverance from this suffering in hope and faith in Christ. Jünger himself seems to have recognized just how far he had gone in "On Pain." Only five years later, *On the Marble Cliffs* (1939) contains passages that can be read as a refutation

36. Ibid., pp. 438–39.

of the metaphysics of pain articulated in "Über den Schmerz."
This change in perspective is said to be a consequence of his
alleged turn to Christian humanism, which culminated in *Der
Friede* (1945), his call on the youth of Europe and the world
for a return to Christendom in response to the nihilism of
totalitarianism.

"On Pain" poses several challenges for a translator. On the
one hand, Jünger makes use of military terminology that,
depending on the context, is not easily translated into English, such as *Material-Schlacht* (battle of *matériel*) or *Rüstung*
(preparation for war). This is no less true for other terms, such
as *Gestalt*, *Sicherheit* (security/safety), or *Entfernung* (detach-
ment/distance), that assume a more systematic role in Jünger's
essay. Here, I have had the luxury of being able to consult earlier
translations of Jünger's writings, such as Michael Hofmann's
Storm of Steel, Joel Golb and Richard Wolin's "Total Mobilization," and Joel Agee's short excerpt from "On Pain."[37] On the
other hand, a further, more serious challenge rests in render-
ing the style or tone of Jünger's essay into English. As befits
his approach to the problem of pain, Jünger's diction and style
aspire to a kind of "noble detachment" in judgment, which
this self-proclaimed "field marshal of ideas" felt was "requisite
for sovereign rule." In this sense, "On Pain" is an expression
of Jünger's famed *désinvolture*. Jünger was no doubt con-
scious of this. In another essay in *Leaves and Stones*, "Praise
of Vowels" ("Lob der Vokale"), Jünger provides insight into

37. See Ernst Jünger, *Storm of Steel*, trans. Michael Hofmann (London;
Penguin, 1996); Ernst Jünger, "Total Mobilization," trans. Joel Golb and
Richard Wolin, in *The Heidegger Controversy: A Critical Reader*, ed. Richard
Wolin (Boston: MIT Press, 1993), pp. 119–39; Ernst Jünger, "Photography
and the 'Second Consciousness': An Excerpt from 'On Pain,'" trans. Joel
Agee, in *Photography in the Modern Era: European Documents and Critical
Writings, 1913–1940*, ed. Christopher Philipps (New York: The Metropolitan
Museum of Modern Art/Aperture, 1989), pp. 207–10.

the mechanics of this style of detachment. Borrowing from the German philologist Jakob Grimm, Jünger speaks of the "masculine ground of consonants" and "feminine ground of vowels"; if the consonant is hard and manly, the vowel is soft and womanly. He also adds here his thoughts on the relation of consonants and vowels, words and sounds to pain:

> Every significant pain, wherever it may be felt, no longer expresses itself through words but through sounds. The sites of birth and death are filled with such sounds. We have perceived them again perhaps in their full strength in war—on the battlefields at night filled by the calls of wounded, in the great military hospitals, and in the petrifying cry of death, the meaning of which no one will fail to hear. The heart senses these sounds differently than words; immediately, it is touched by both warmth and coldness alike. Human beings become very similar here; through the great pain the uniqueness of the person who feels pain is destroyed. So too are the special qualities of voice destroyed. Consonants are scorched; the sounds of utmost pain have the nature of pure vowels.[38]

In the original German, "On Pain" has a cold and unforgiving quality, despite moments where the bestiality of the modern age seem to haunt Jünger like the cries of wounded on the battlefield. It is an essay more of "consonants" and "words" than of "vowels" and "sounds." It is literally "*Über*" *den Schmerz*, i.e., as if seeking to surmount, with the stress on "*Beyond* the Pain" or "*Over* the Pain." The challenge of translating this essay thus lies in capturing Jünger's embrace of silence amidst a "whole creation" that "groaneth and travaileth in pain."

David C. Durst

38. Ernst Jünger, "Lob der Vokale," in *Blätter und Steine*, p. 60.

On Pain

Of all animals that serve as nourishment to man, lobster must suffer the most torturous death, for it is set in cold water on a hot flame.

Cookbook for Households of All Estates, Berlin 1848

Does a little booby cry for any ache? The mother scolds him in this fashion: "What a coward to cry for a trifling pain! What will you do when your arm is cut off in battle? What when you are called upon to commit harakiri?"

Inazo Notibé, *Bushido*, Tokyo 2560 (1900)

1.

There are several great and unalterable dimensions that show a man's stature. *Pain* is one of them. It is the most difficult in a series of trials one is accustomed to call life. An examination dealing with pain is no doubt unpopular; yet it is not only revealing in its own right, but it can also shed light on a series of questions preoccupying us at the present. Pain is one of the keys to unlock man's innermost being as well as the world. Whenever one approaches the points where man proves himself to be equal or superior to pain, one gains access to the sources of his power and the secret hidden behind his dominion. Tell me your relation to pain, and I will tell you who you are!

Pain as a measure of man is unalterable, but what can be altered is the way he confronts it. Man's relation to pain changes with every significant shift in fundamental belief. This relation is in no way set; rather, it eludes our knowledge, and yet is the

1

best benchmark by which to discern a race. We can observe this clearly today, since we have a novel and peculiar relation to pain in a world without binding norms.

Through examination of this new kind of relation to pain, we now intend to secure an elevated point of surveillance, from which we may be able to catch sight of things still imperceptible on the ground. Our question is: What role does pain play in the new race we have called the *worker* that is now making its appearance on the historical stage?[1]

Concerning the inner form of this investigation, we are striving for the effect of a bombshell bursting with delayed action, and we promise the attentive reader that he shall not be spared.

2.

Let us direct our attention first of all toward the peculiar mechanics and economy of pain! The ear becomes anxious when it hears the words *pain* and *mechanics* together—and this is because the individual has a desire to situate pain in the realm of chance, in a zone one can avoid and evade or at the very least need not be subject to according to the laws of necessity.

But if one musters up the inner distance necessary for examination of this object, such as the standpoint of a doctor or a spectator in the galleries watching the gushing blood of gladiators from foreign lands, one soon senses that pain has a sure and ineluctable hold. Nothing is more certain and unavoidable than pain; it resembles life's inescapable shadow or a gristmill grinding the grain ever finer and with ever more incisive rotations.

---

1. Ernst Jünger's *Der Arbeiter: Herrschaft und Gestalt* (*The Worker: Mastery and Form*) was published in the autumn of 1932 by the Hanseatische Verlagsanstalt in Hamburg.

The ineluctability of pain's hold stands out with particular clarity in the observation of smaller processes of life condensed into short time-intervals. The insect at our feet, winding its way through the thicket as through the depths of a jungle, seems threatened to an unimaginable degree. Its tiny path resembles a train of terrifying encounters. On both sides it confronts a vast arsenal of obstacles and trenches. And yet this path is but a likeness of our own. Surely we are apt to forget this relation in times of refuge; but we are reminded of it immediately whenever the elementary zone comes into sight. We are embedded inextricably in this zone, and we cannot evade it through any kind of optical illusion. We feast and stroll like Sinbad the Sailor with his wayward followers on the back of an enormous fish he mistakes for an island.

The chant *Media in vita* springs from a sentiment aware of this threat.[2] We also possess exceptional images of how life is surrounded and engulfed by pain in the impressive paintings of Hieronymus Bosch, Brueghel, and Cranach, whose significance we begin to appreciate again today and which only a short time ago were considered absurd inventions.[3] These paintings are more modern than one believes, and it is not by accident that technical skill plays such a significant role in

2. *Media vita in morte sumus* ("In the middle of life we are surrounded by death") is the beginning of a Latin antiphon that in the Middle Ages was erroneously ascribed to Notker of St. Gall (ca. 840–912), a musician and Benedictine monk at the Abbey of St. Gall, in St. Gallen, Switzerland.

3. Hieronymus Bosch (1450–1516) was an Early Netherlandish painter famous for his triptychs and portrayals of scenes from hell, as given, for instance, in *The Garden of Earthly Delights* and *The Last Judgment*, both from 1504; Pieter Brueghel the Elder (ca. 1525–1569) was a Netherlandish Renaissance painter known for his peasant scenes and also his images of death in *The Triumph of Death* and *Dull Gret*, both dated to 1562; Lucas Cranach the Elder (1472–1553) was a German painter and printmaker famous for his portraits of Martin Luther and other prominent figures of the Reformation era.

them. Many of Bosch's paintings, with their nocturnal con-
flagrations and infernal flues, resemble industrial landscapes
in full operation, and Cranach's *Great Inferno*, on display in
Berlin, contains a complete array of technical instruments.[4]
One of the often recurring motifs is a rolling canopy, with a
large, shining knife jutting out of the opening. The sight of
such devices evokes a special kind of horror; they are symbols
of a mechanically disguised assault that is colder and more
rapacious than any other.

3.

Pain's disregard for our system of values greatly increases its
hold on life. The emperor who, when urged to remove himself
from the line of fire, responded by asking whether one had
ever heard of an emperor falling in battle, exposed himself to
one of those errors to which we all too willingly succumb. No
human situation is secure against pain. Our children's tales
close with passages about heroes who, after having overcome
many dangers, live out their lives in peace and happiness. We
hear such assurances with pleasure, for it is comforting for
us to learn about a place removed from pain. Yet, in truth,
life is without any such satisfying end, as is evidenced by the
fragmentary character of most great novels, which are either
incomplete or crowned by an artificial conclusion. Even *Faust*
closes with this sort of contrived literary device.[5]

4. The reference is to Cranach's triptych *Das Jüngste Gericht* (*The Last
Judgment*) (1520), which Jünger could see in the Kaiser Friedrich Museum
in Berlin during his residence in the city between 1927 and 1933. The triptych is almost an exact copy of Bosch's altarpiece *The Last Judgment*, from
1504.

5. Johann Wolfgang von Goethe's *Faust: The Tragedy, Part I* was published in 1808, and *Faust: The Tragedy, Part II* appeared in print shortly after
his death in 1832.

The fact that pain repudiates our values is easily hidden in times of peace. Yet we already begin to reel when a joyful, wealthy, or powerful man is stricken by the most ordinary afflictions. The sickness of Friedrich III, who died of routine throat cancer, evoked an almost incredible sense of astonishment.[6] A very similar sentiment can seize us when, observing a dissection, we encounter human organs indiscriminately perforated or covered with malignant tumors, indicating a long, individual path of suffering. The seeds of destruction are indifferent to whether they destroy the mind of a numskull or a genius. The scurrilous, yet significant, verse of Shakespeare speaks to this sentiment:

> Imperious Caesar, dead and turn'd to clay,
> Might stop a hole to keep the wind away.[7]

Schiller, too, elaborates on this fundamental idea in his "Stroll under the Linden Trees."[8]

During times we are apt to call unusual, the indiscriminate nature of this threat is even more apparent. In war, when shells fly past our bodies at high speeds, we sense clearly that no level of intelligence, virtue, or fortitude is strong enough to deflect them, not even by a hair. To the extent this threat increases, doubt concerning the validity of our values forces itself upon us. The mind tends toward a catastrophic interpretation of

6. In 1888, Ernst Georg Jünger (1868–1943), Ernst Jünger's father, worked in the Lucaeschen Apothecary on Unter den Linden in the heart of Berlin. One of his responsibilities included preparing the medical prescriptions for Kaiser Friedrich III, who after only 99 days as German Emperor died of throat cancer. See here Heimo Schwilk's biography of Jünger, *Ernst Jünger: Ein Jahrhundertleben: Die Biographie* (Munich: Piper Verlag, 2007), pp. 26–27.

7. William Shakespeare, *The Tragedy of Hamlet, Prince of Denmark*, act 5, scene 1.

8. Friedrich Schiller, "Der Spaziergang unter den Linden" (1782).

things wherever it sees everything called into question. Among the questions of eternal debate is the great clash between the Neptunists and Vulcanists—while the past century, in which the idea of progress predominated, can be characterized as a Neptunistic age, we tend increasingly toward Vulcanic views.[9]

Such a tendency can be seen best in the particular predilections of the mind; a predisposition to a sense of ruin has its proper place here. It has not only conquered broad domains of science, but it also explains the lure of countless sects. Apocalyptic visions spread. Historical analysis begins to investigate the potential for a complete collapse to take place internally through deadly cultural diseases or externally through the assault of the most foreign and unmerciful forces, such as the "colored" races.[10] In this connection the mind feels itself drawn toward the image of powerful empires perishing in their prime. The rapid destruction of the South American cultures forces us to admit that even the greatest civilizations we know are not

9. The controversy between Neptunism and Vulcanism (or Plutonism) took place around the turn of the nineteenth century. Neptunism was a geological theory developed by the German professor of mining Abraham Werner (1749–1815) in the eighteenth century. He argued that rocks were formed through the crystallization of minerals in the oceans of the earth; hence, this theory was named after Neptune, the Roman name for the Greek god of the sea, Poseidon. In end of the eighteenth century, the Scottish geologist James Hutton (1726–1797), often considered the father of modern geology, formulated an opposing theory maintaining that the source of rocks on the surface of the Earth was to be traced to volcanic activity; hence, it was named after Pluto, the Roman god of the underworld. Goethe's *Faust: The Tragedy, Part II* contains dialogues on Neptunism and Plutonism (*Faust: The Tragedy, Part II*, act 2, scene 6). Goethe supported Neptunism, which would in the course of the nineteenth century be rejected in favor of Vulcanism.

10. The reference to "colored races" evokes the name of Oswald Spengler (1860–1936), an intellectual mentor for Jünger, and Spengler's speculations on the threat he argued that the "colored races" represent to Western civilization in *Man and Technics* (1931) and *Hour of Decision* (1933).

assured safe development. In such times, the primordial memory of the lost Atlantis recurs. Archeology is actually a science dedicated to pain; in the layers of the earth, it uncovers empire after empire, of which we no longer even know the names. The mourning that takes hold of us at such sites is extraordinary, and it is perhaps in no account of the world portrayed more vividly than in the powerful and mysterious tale about the *City of Brass*. In this desolate city surrounded by deserts, the Emir Musa reads the words on a tablet made of iron of China: "For I possessed four thousand bay horses in a stable; and I married a thousand damsels, of the daughters of Kings, high-bosomed virgins, like moons; and I was blessed with a thousand children, like stern lions; and I lived a thousand years, happy in mind and heart; and I amassed riches such as the Kings of the regions of the earth were unable to procure, and I imagined that my enjoyments would continue without failure. But I was not aware when there alighted among us the terminator of delights and the separator of companions, the desolator of abodes and the ravager of inhabited mansions, the destroyer of the great and the small and the infants and the children and the mothers. We had resided in this palace in security until the event decreed by the Lord of all creatures, the Lord of the heavens and the Lord of the earths, befell us." Further, on a table of yellow onyx were graven the words: "Upon this table have eaten a thousand one-eyed Kings, and a thousand Kings each sound in both eyes. All of them have quitted the world, and taken up their abode in the burial-grounds and the graves."[11]

11. "The Story of the City of Brass," in *Stories from the Thousand and One Nights*, trans. Edward William Lane, rev. Stanley Lane-Poole, in Charles W. Eliot, ed., *The Harvard Classics*, vol. 16 (New York: P. F. Collier & Son, 1909–14). Jünger's interest in "The Story of the City of Brass" and Emir Musa began in his ninth year as a child and was further influenced by his friend Rudolf Schlichter, one of the most important representatives of the *Neue Sachlichkeit* (New Objectivity) movement of painters in Germany

Astronomy vies with the pessimistic view of history, which
projects the mark of destruction onto planetary spaces. News
reports about the "red spot" on Jupiter stir in us a peculiar
sense of anxiety.[12] The cognitive eye is clouded by our most
secret desires and fears. In the sciences one sees this best in the
sect-like character that one of its branches, such as the "Cosmic Ice Theory," suddenly attains.[13] The recent attention to the
enormous craters, which apparently resulted from the impact
of meteoric projectiles on our earth's crust, is also typical.

Finally, war, which has from time immemorial formed a
part of apocalyptic visions, also offers imagination a wealth of
material. Depictions of future clashes were popular well before
the World War; and they again today make up a voluminous
literature. The peculiar nature of this literature is rooted in the
focus on total destruction; man grows accustomed to the sight
of future expanses of ruin, where wholesale slaughter triumphs
in endless domination. We are dealing here with something
more than literary moods. This can be seen in the actual

during the Weimar Republic. See here Schlichter's sketches *Die Messingstadt*
(*The City of Brass*) and *Emir Musa reitet in die Messingstadt ein* (*Emir Musa
Rides into the City of Brass*). See also *Ernst Jünger, Rudolf Schlichter: Briefe
1935–1955*, ed. Dirk Heißerer (Stuttgart: Klett-Cotta, 1997). Schlichter also
did a sketch of the lost city of Atlantis, entitled *Atlantis vor dem Untergang*
(*Atlantis Before Ruin*).

12. The "great red spot" is a continuing anti-cyclonic storm on the
planet Jupiter, which was first observed by telescope by the Italian astrono-
mer Giovanni Domenico Cassini around 1665. The nature of the great red
spot remained an object of speculation for astronomers until the Voyager
mission in 1979.

13. The *Welteislehre* (Cosmic Ice Theory) was a theory propounded by
the Austrian engineer Hans Hörbiger (1860–1931). In *Glazial-Kosmogo-
nie*, published in 1913, Hörbiger maintained that existence is based on an
eternal struggle between fire and ice, a belief that had parallels with Norse
mythology. Houston Stewart Chamberlain promoted Hörbiger's *Welteislehre*, and during the Third Reich, the *Welteislehre* became official Nazi
policy in cosmology.

preventive measures already in full gear. A dark foreboding danger overshadows life, which is reflected in the way all the civilized states are currently taking precautionary steps against chemical warfare. In his noteworthy history of the plague in London, Defoe describes how before the actual outbreak of the Black Death, alongside the renowned plague doctors, an army of magicians, quacks, sectarians, and statisticians poured into the city as a vanguard of the infernal wind. Situations of this kind repeat themselves over and over again, for the eye of man naturally searches for spaces of shelter and safety at the sight of pain so inescapable and antithetical to his values.[14] In sensing the uncertainty and vulnerability of life as a whole, man increasingly needs to turn his sights to a space removed from the unlimited rule and prevailing power of pain.

4.

This need seems especially striking when contrasted with the hopes of the age of widespread security, whose values are still fully familiar to us today. The Last Man, as Nietzsche prophesied, is already history, and even if we have not yet reached the year 2000, it seems certain it will look entirely different than depicted in Bellamy's utopia.[15] We find ourselves in a situation of wanderers traipsing along endlessly over a frozen sea, whose surface begins to break up into great sheets of ice due to a change in climate. The surface of abstract ideas likewise starts to become brittle, and the depth of the substance, which was always present, shines dimly through the cracks and crevices.

---

14. Daniel Defoe, *A Journal of the Plague Year* (1722).

15. The reference here is to the American author Edward Bellamy (1850–1898) and his utopian novel *Looking Backward: 2000–1887*, which appeared in 1888.

In this situation, the biased belief that reason can conquer pain loses its allure. This belief is not only a characteristic feature of forces allied with the Enlightenment, but it has also produced a long series of practical measures typical for the human spirit of the past century, such as—to name just a few—the abolition of torture and the slave trade, the discovery of electricity, vaccination against measles, narcosis, the system of insurance, and a whole world of technical and political conveniences. We still appreciate all these celebrated dates of progress, and wherever one, let's say, mocks them, it is due to a romantic dandyism, which flatters itself haughtily as a finer spirit amidst a boundlessly democratic lifestyle. Our recognition of these achievements already lacks the noteworthy cult-like characteristic still familiar to us from our fathers. Born in full enjoyment of all these blessings now taken for granted, it seems to us as if in truth rather little has changed.

Since the War's end, the denial of pain as a necessary facet of life has experienced a late revival. These years display a strange mix of barbarity and humanity; they resemble an archipelago where an isle of vegetarians exists right next to an island of cannibals. An extreme pacifism side by side with an enormous intensification of war preparations, luxurious prisons next to squalid quarters for the unemployed, the abolition of capital punishment by day whilst the Whites and the Reds cut each other's throats by night—all this is thoroughly fairytale-like and reflects a sordid world in which the semblance of security is preserved in a string of hotel foyers.

5.

The memory of the nineteenth century has already given rise to a late romantic literature. Today a similar melancholy is attached to Napoleon III's France, Wilhelmine Germany, the Victorian era, and the colonial life of whites, just as was earlier attached to the period before 1789, of which Talleyrand once remarked that no one born since knows what life is.[16]

This melancholy seems warranted if one takes into account the personal liberty and degree to which pain was formerly kept at bay for the individual. The amount of security is indeed extraordinary; it is produced by a convergence of propitious circumstances. Ever since the religious conflicts ceased, the new nation-states have found themselves in a state of relative complacency assuring a measure of social stability. Moreover, since the Third Estate's victory has become self-evident to all, domestic politics has been characterized by a high degree of predictability. The bourgeoisie's norms are accepted by the older estates as well as by classes striving for upward mobility. Progress combines the economic conquest of the globe, which magnetically draws in the most distant lands, with ridding the world of all prejudices that can cause pain.

This widespread state of security, as it immediately struck Dostoevsky upon his short stay in Paris, shells out shares of good fortune to the widest reaches.[17] The transformation of things into abstract ideas, such as goods into money or natural

16. The Talleyrand quote referred to here is from his *Confessions*: "Celui qui n'a pas vécu au dix-huitième siècle avant la Révolution ne connaît pas la douceur de vivre" ("Those who haven't lived in the eighteenth century before the Revolution will never be able to know the sweetness of life"). See Charles-Maurice de Talleyrand-Périgord, *La Confession de Talleyrand*, ed. Albert de Broglie (Paris: L. Sauvaitre, 1891).

17. The reference here is to Dostoevsky's depiction of Parisian comforts, conveniences, and security during his trip to Western Europe during 1862. See Dostoevsky, *Winter Notes on Summer Impressions*, trans. Richard Lee Renfield (New York: McGraw-Hill, 1955), chap. 5, pp. 87f. and 105ff. Dostoevsky's book appeared in Germany around 1930 under the title *Winterliche Bemerkungen über sommerliche Eindrücke* in a collection of short novels and short stories (Dostojewskij, *Das Dorf Stepantschikowo: Kleine Romane und Erzählungen, 1859–1865*, trans. Gregor Jarcho [Berlin: Büchergilde Gutenberg, ca. 1930]).

human ties into juridical relations, brings an extraordinary ease and freedom of movement to life. This ease is enhanced by the fact that the flair and ability for artistic enjoyment has not yet been completely lost. On the contrary, the decrease in creative powers produces a special empathy with traditional values; the third generation of the bourgeoisie is a generation of collectors, experts, historians, and travelers. Individual love has reached a stage that to a certain degree has outstripped the *liaisons dangereuses*, since the capacity for pleasure has been retained whilst its inhibitions have been brushed aside. Tragic endings, as in *Paul and Virginia* or in *Werther* or even still in *Madame Bovary*, are pointless—the artist classic for his depictions of late-bourgeois amorous relationships is Maupassant.[18] Today we already sense in reading these depictions how the charm of these intimate secrets and revelations is lost on us, and the sight of a film played around the turn of the century, with female fashions tailored so very much to pleasure and so little to sport or work, transports us into a state of historical illusion.

The *breadth* of people partaking of goods and pleasures is a sign of prosperity. Perhaps most symbolic are the grand cafés, in the halls of which one is fond of replicating the styles of the Rococo, Empire, and Biedermeier. They can be called the true palaces of democracy. Here one senses the dream-like, painless, and oddly agitated ease that fills the air like a narcotic. On the streets it is striking how the masses are dressed in such undeniably poor taste, yet in a uniform and "respectable" fashion. Bare and blatant poverty is rarely seen. The individual is

18. Jacques-Henri Bernardin de Saint-Pierre, *Paul and Virginia* (1787); Goethe, *The Sorrows of Young Werther* (1774); Gustave Flaubert, *Madame Bovary* (1857). Jünger translated Guy de Maupassant's study on ether; see "Vom Äther," translated on September 8, 1919, from Maupassant's "Rêves," in Jünger, *Sämtliche Werke* (Stuttgart: Klett-Cotta, 1983–2004), Bd. 22, pp. 773ff.

greeted by a wealth of conveniences, such as the path paved for education and a career choice of preference, the free market of labor, the contractual character of almost all social ties, and the unrestricted freedom of movement. The potential for conflict is thereby greatly reduced. What is more, a quality of pure convenience is still an integral part of the fabulous expansion of technical means—it all seems designed to light up, warm, move, entertain, and deliver streams of gold.

The prophecy of the Last Man has found rapid fulfillment. It is accurate—except for the assertion that the Last Man lives longest.[19] His age already lies behind us.

6.

No claim, however, is more certain than the one pain has on life. Where people are spared pain, social stability is produced according to the laws of a very specific economy, and, by a turn of phrase, one can speak of a "cunning of pain" that never fails to reach its aim. At the sight of this state of widespread comfort, one is prompted to ask immediately where the burden is borne. As a rule one will not have to go far to uncover the pain. Indeed, even the individual is not fully free from pain in this joyful state of security. The artificial check on the elementary forces might be able to prevent violent clashes and to ward off shadows, but it cannot stop the dispersed light with which pain permeates life. The vessel, sealed off from pain's full flow, is filled drop by drop. Boredom is nothing other than the dissolution of pain in time.

Pain's hidden influence also comes to light in the feeling of embitterment. The soul's pain is of an inferior kind;[20] it is

---

19. The reference is to Friedrich Nietzsche, *Thus Spoke Zarathustra*, "Zarathustra's Prologue," sect. 5.

20. Jünger's note: "That is to say, insofar as it belongs to the characteristic of pain that it concerns reality in its full scope. Within a system of terms

among the sicknesses causing a rejection of sacrifice. Perhaps nothing is therefore more characteristic of the turn of the century than the predominance of psychology as a science. It bears the most intimate relation to pain, as is confirmed by its advance into the field of medical science. A sense of deep mistrust also has its place here: the feeling of being demoralized by malicious ploys, whether in relation to economic, intellectual, moral, or racial matters. This feeling pours out into a state of general indictment—into a literature of the blind, who are constantly in search of those responsible.

Pain confronts us in an even more terrifying way wherever it reaches the sources of *procreation*. Here, all significant life-forces are in a state of suffocation—the heights of rank and the depths of pain stand in immediate relation to one another. Here, every kind of complacency is suspicious, for under the sway of abstract ideas no one can be content who maintains a relation to the essential things of life. It therefore comes as no surprise that in these times, genius, i.e., maintaining the highest vigor, is taken to be a form of madness, just as giving birth is portrayed as a sickness or the soldier is no longer distinguished from the butcher. Whoever considers torture a medieval institution will soon learn a different lesson when he delves into the *Ecce Homo*, Baudelaire's correspondence, or one of the other terrifying documents handed down to us in such great numbers.[21] In a world full of inferior values, every order of greatness is dragged through the dirt, and the most extreme sphere of suffering, which the dim-witted can venture

---

where the soul and reality are synonymous, there is thus the pain of the soul, as is the case in Augustine: 'For it is the soul not the body, which is pained' (*City of God*, bk. 21, chap. 3)."

21. The reference is to Nietzsche's *Ecce Homo: How One Becomes What One Is*, which was written in 1888 and first published posthumously in 1908.

to see, is symbolized by Caspar Hauser and Dreyfus.[22] The spirit's betrayal of the law of existence is reflected most incisively in the pain of individuals of stature. The same is true for momentous occasions altogether, such as youth when stripped of its "ardent element," as Hölderlin laments in his poem "To the Intelligent Counselor."[23]

When one considers pain's penetration into the realm of procreation, one cannot forget the assault on the unborn, which typifies the simultaneously weak and bestial character of the Last Man. To be sure, a mind incapable of differentiating between war and murder or crime and disease will definitely select in territorial struggles *the* safest and most pitiful method of killing. For a defense lawyer, one only sees the suffering of the plaintiff, but not that of the unprotected and silent.

The nature of this security therefore lies in the fact that pain is marginalized in favor of a run-of-the-mill complacency. Alongside this spatial economy, there is a temporal one, consisting of the sum of pain that remains unclaimed and amasses as hidden capital accruing compound interest. The threat grows with every artificial increase in the barrier separating man from the elementary forces.

7.

What does the growth of sensitivity actually mean, as it can be observed for over the past 150 years? In vain we try to transport ourselves into a world where the seventeen-year-old Origen

22. Caspar Hauser (1812–1833) was a foundling discovered on the streets of Nuremberg, Germany, in 1824, whose unknown birth and death became legend. Alfred Dreyfus (1859–1935) was a French artillery officer of Jewish descent, whose trial, conviction in 1894 on charges of treason, and cover-up of his innocence by the French army led to a political drama known as the Dreyfus Affair; it sparked debate on antisemitism in modern France.
23. The reference is to the poem "An die klugen Ratgeber" by the German poet Friedrich Hölderlin (1770–1843).

was able to beseech his imprisoned father not to desist from martyrdom out of concern for his family, or where women first took the lives of their children and then themselves, which was the typical spectacle after an assault on a Germanic laager.[24]

Historical accounts of this kind demonstrate that the estimation of pain is not the same throughout time. There are apparently attitudes that enable man to become detached from the realms of life where pain reigns as absolute master. This detachment emerges wherever man is able to treat the space through which he experiences pain, i.e., the body, as an object. Of course, this presupposes a command center, which regards the body as a distant outpost that can be deployed and sacrificed in battle. Henceforth, all measures are designed to master pain, not to avoid it. The heroic and cultic world presents an entirely different relation to pain than does the world of sensitivity. While in the latter, as we saw, it is a matter of marginalizing pain and sheltering life from it, in the former the point is to integrate pain and organize life in such a way that one is always armed against it. Here, too, pain plays a significant, but no doubt opposite, role. This is because life strives incessantly to stay in contact with pain. Indeed, discipline means nothing other than this, whether it is of the priestly-ascetic kind directed toward abnegation or of the warlike-heroic kind directed toward hardening oneself

24. In his *Church History*, Eusebius reports of Origen's letter to his father on martyrdom: "But, as there was nothing else that he could do, and his zeal beyond his age would not suffer him to be quiet, he sent to his father an encouraging letter on martyrdom, in which he exhorted him, saying, 'Take heed not to change your mind on our account.' This may be recorded as the first evidence of Origen's youthful wisdom and of his genuine love for piety." Eusebius, *Church History*, in Philip Schaff and Henry Wace, eds., *Church History, Life of Constantine the Great, and Oration in Praise of Constantine*, trans. Philip Schaff (Peabody, MA: Hendrickson Publishers, 1995), bk. 6, chap. 2, pt. 6.

like steel. In both cases, it is a matter of maintaining complete control over life, so that at any hour of the day it can serve a higher calling. The central question concerning the rank of present values can be answered by determining to what extent the body can be treated as an object.

The secret of modern sensitivity is that it corresponds to a world in which the body is itself the highest value. This observation explains why modern sensitivity relates to pain as a power to be avoided at all cost, because here pain confronts the body not as an outpost but as the main force and essential core of life.

8.

Today, we can say with some certainty that the world of the self-gratifying and self-critical individual is over and that its system of values, if no doubt still widespread, has been overthrown in all decisive points or refuted by its very own consequences. There is no dearth of efforts to secure a world in which a new and more powerful system of values prevails. However much these efforts, taken separately, are to be welcomed, a real breakthrough has yet to be achieved. The reason for this is that a command center capable of treating the assault of pain in a purely tactical way cannot be produced by artificial means. Exertions of the will are in particular insufficient here, since it is a matter of natural superiority. One cannot just artificially cultivate a "heroic worldview" or proclaim it *ex cathedra*. This heroic worldview is granted to the hero solely by a right of birth, and it is inevitably diminished when it filters down to the masses as an abstract ideal. The same is true for race altogether; a race exists and is recognized through its actions. A total state likewise presupposes the existence of at least one single total human being, and the purely moral will begets in the best case a total bureaucracy. In relation to cultic associations, this connection becomes even more evident; the advent of a god is independent of human effort.

This assessment is significant to the extent that it contains a standard of judgment regarding the preparation for war. In order to make clear just how high the demands on preparedness have become, consider a practical example. Recently, a story circulated in the newspapers about a new torpedo that the Japanese navy is apparently developing. This weapon has an astounding feature. It is no longer guided mechanically but by a human device—to be precise, by a human being at the helm, who is locked into a tiny compartment and regarded as a technical component of the torpedo as well as its actual intelligence.

The idea behind this peculiar organic construction drives the logic of the technical world a small step forward by transforming man in an unprecedented way into one of its component parts. If one enlarges upon this thought, one soon realizes that it is no longer considered a curiosity once achieved on a larger social scale, i.e., when one disposes over a breed of resolute men obedient to authority. Manned planes can then be constructed as airborne missiles, which from great heights can dive down to strike with lethal accuracy the nerve centers of enemy resistance. The result is a breed of men that can be sent off to war as cannon fodder. This would no doubt be the most dreadful symbol of the right to sovereign rule imaginable. Here, all potential for good luck is eliminated with mathematical certainty, presupposing of course that one does not have an entirely different conception of luck. We confront this entirely different conception of luck, however, when we hear that General Nogi, one of the few figures of our times and a man worthy of being called a "hero," received "with deep satisfaction" the news that his son had fallen in battle.[25]

25. Nogi Maresuke (1849–1912) was a prominent general in the Imperial Japanese Army, who studied military strategy in Germany and commanded

To link another thought to the idea of the human projectile, it is obvious that with such a stance man is superior to every imaginable multitude of individuals. His superiority, of course, is still given even when not armed with explosives, for we are not dealing here with superiority over human beings but over the space in which the law of pain rules. This superiority is the highest; it bears within itself all other forms of superiority.

Of course, our ethos is not suited for such kinds of behavior, which surface at best in situations of nihilistic extreme. In one of Joseph Conrad's prophetic novels, which portrays a Russian revolutionary's activities in London, an anarchist appears who has thought through to the very last consequence the idea of individual liberty and, in order to never submit to force, never goes without a bomb by his side.[26] He can set it off with a rubber ball he clutches in his hand, if he is threatened with arrest.

9.

The pretensions of arbitrary convictions are inadequate to judge the situation today. Words change nothing. They are at best signs of change. Change, however, takes place in reality, and it becomes most clearly visible when we seek to understand this change without prior value judgment.

Elsewhere we described the current transformation of the individual into the type of the worker.[27] In relation to pain,

the Japanese Third Army in the Russo-Japanese war of 1904–5. Nogi's eldest son died while serving with the Japanese Second Army at the battle of Nan-shan on the Liaodong Peninsula of what was then referred to as southern east-Manchuria, now northeastern China. Nogi's second son was killed in the Siege of Port Arthur, which lasted from August 1904 to January 1905. With the fall of Port Arthur to Japanese forces, Nogi became a hero.

26. The reference is to the character known simply as "The Professor" in Conrad's *The Secret Agent* (1907).

27. The reference is to Jünger's *Der Arbeiter* (*The Worker*), published in 1932.

this transformation eliminates the zone of sensitivity from life, and, consequently, it is initially felt as a loss. Individual liberty and the opportunities for free movement it has brought to the most diverse spheres of life belong in this zone. Restrictions on liberty constitute special cases, the most significant example of which was universal military conscription. The relation between liberty and its restriction, like many others, has already reversed itself to a great extent; the new tendency regards duty as life-defining for the human condition. The inevitable nature of such reversals can be seen clearly in Germany, where they prevailed against both a general state of domestic exhaustion and restrictions imposed by international treaties.

A second zone of sensitivity is devastated by the assault on liberal education. The effects of this assault are much less apparent. This has various reasons, but the most important one is that we continue to idolize ideas that artificially support the principles of liberal education, especially the idea of culture. Yet this changes nothing on the ground, because the assault on individual liberty inevitably involves an assault on liberal education. This becomes apparent when we are forced to deny the right to free inquiry. Free inquiry is impossible wherever its essential purpose is preparation for war, because, like a blind man, free inquiry opens all doors arbitrarily. Yet today the only door to unlock is the one to power. Free inquiry is pointless once it becomes clear what should be known and what should not. Inquiry is assigned here its tasks by virtue of higher laws that predetermine its methodology and focus. Of course, it is still embarrassing for us to think that knowledge should be restricted, but we must admit that this has been the case in every truly decisive moment of history. Herodotus offers us the example of a geographer and ethnologist who is aware of the limits of his science. And Copernicus's revolution was only possible because the capacity for supreme authority had already been lost. We also find ourselves without a supreme authority. What is taken for the supreme authority today is but a surrogate, and this needs further investigation. If a supreme authority were truly given, the pain we are caused by restrictions on knowledge would immediately disappear.

We can assume that in the future this new assessment of the value of free inquiry as the pillar of liberal education will correspond to a comprehensive transformation in the organization of educational practices as a whole. We are now in an experimental stage. Nevertheless, we can predict with some certainty that education will become more limited and more focused, as can be observed wherever the training of man as a type rather than as an individual takes precedence. This is true for military academies as well as seminaries, where from the outset rigorous discipline governs the entire course of training. This is no less true for education in vocational professions and the crafts. By contrast, the model of individual growth is articulated in the *Confessions*, which gave rise to a wealth of novels of self-cultivation and development.[28] It still sounds strange that education is becoming specialized "again," even though by all appearances we are already far along on this path. Until just recently everyone, at least in principle, had the chance to enter the highest levels of education. This is no longer the case today. We observe, for instance, that in many countries certain fields of study are now closed off to the younger generations from social strata assigned a lower level of reliability. The existence of *numerus clausus*, as applied to individual professions, institutions of higher education, or universities, is also indicative of a determination to cut off education right from the start to specific social classes, such as the academic proletariat, based on national interest. Of course, these are just isolated symptoms, but they nevertheless suggest

28. The reference is to the *Confessions* of Jean-Jacques Rousseau (1712–1778), which was first published posthumously in 1782.

that the free choice of a profession is no longer an unquestioned social arrangement.

The possibility of specialized training in turn presupposes the existence of a supreme authority. This kind of training can only make sense if the state appears as the representative of the total character of work. Enormous undertakings, such as the resettlement of entire portions of a population to a colony, are only imaginable within this framework. These kinds of undertakings even involve assigning professions to individuals prior to their birth. One can also note the restrictions on liberal education in the military training now already commencing in the grade schools in most civilized states.

Undertakings of this kind naturally have an impact on the human condition or, stated better, are indications that this condition is beginning to change. We detect in all these examples an explicit or implicit penchant for discipline. We described discipline as the way man maintains contact with pain. It therefore cannot surprise us that today one encounters faces ever more often that until just recently were only to be found in the last recesses of vocational training, especially in the Prussian Army, this great stronghold of heroic values. In the liberal world, what one considered a "good" face was, properly speaking, the delicate face—nervous, pliant, changing, and open to the most diverse kinds of influences and impulses. By contrast, the disciplined face is resolute; it possesses clear direction, and it is single-minded, objective, and unyielding. One immediately notices by every kind of rigorous training how the imposition of firm and impersonal rules and regulations is reflected in the hardening of the face.

10.

This new kind of relation to pain is not only evident in the individual but also in the formations he strives for. When traveling today through the countries of Europe, whether they are in a peculiar transitional phase to a one-party state or just aspiring to it, one is especially struck by the fact that the role of the uniform has become even more important than in the age of universal military conscription. The common traits of attire extend not only to all age groups but even to the different sexes, and they evoke a curious impression that the discovery of the worker is accompanied by the discovery of a third sex. But this is a topic of its own. Be that as it may, the uniform always incorporates the character of armor, a claim to be armed in a special way against the assault of pain. This is apparent in the fact that one can look at a dead person in uniform with greater indifference than, let us say, a civilian shot dead in street-fighting. In photographic images that, taken in flight at high altitudes, capture the sight of massive deployments of troops, one sees in the depths below orderly squares and human columns, magical figures whose innermost meaning is directed to the exorcism of pain.

Visions of this kind possess something immediately intelligible. One has the same impression when flying over a city where an old fortification's geometric shape has been maintained in the midst of bewildering street traffic. It is not only in the field of architecture, in which there are in principle only two metaphysical edifices, that cultic and warlike formations share a resemblance to crystal formations. On certain occasions, these cultic and warlike formations intersect in an astonishing way, such as at the Battle of Lepanto, where the Turkish fleet organized itself for attack in the form of a crescent and the Christian fleet in the form of a cross.[29]

We can assume that in the future not only will our architecture reconnect with battle plans, as we can already see

---

29. The reference is to the Battle of Lepanto of 1571.

in attempts to adapt building structures to the threat of air and chemical-weapons attacks; conversely, the war front will assume specific formations based on the mass character of the era of universal military conscription. Here we note that, while fortification walls were being demolished and churches transmogrified into museums, urban architecture strangely enough still revealed clear traits of preparation for war and defense. Anyone entering the banking districts at the heart of today's cities will be convinced by this assertion. One is struck by the instinct that conceived of these strongholds in such a seemingly secure space, built of otherwise unused squared stone, with iron-barred windows and protected with steel-plated inside vaults. Here one also grasps the meaning of that peculiar, festive mood that radiates a demonic light throughout the ostentatious cashier halls. It reflects a situation where, if one would grant a person a magic wish, a dream of happiness and life without pain, no other image would be evoked than the magic number "One Million."

Meanwhile we have learned a hard lesson concerning the relative degree of security that money provides.[30] The years in which each person could call himself a millionaire are not far behind us, and whoever today expresses a wish for a million would also be required to stipulate that this presupposes no new inflation or that the money is to be spent in one of the smaller neutral states.

The masses have also turned out to have a similar, deceptive standing relying on many presuppositions, and this returns us to our actual topic. One of the kindred characteristics of free-floating money and the free-floating masses is that they not only do *not* afford protection against the real assault of pain,

---

30. The reference here is to the period of hyperinflation between 1922 and 1923, during the Weimar Republic.

but on the contrary they attract ruin with magnetic force at the moment that life nears the elementary zone of pain.

When one grows up thinking in a specific way, one tends to consider the ideas one uses as realities. The masses are nothing other than an abstract idea, and the act by which a number of people is transformed into such a multitude is convincing only in its own allotted space. Here, however, it is difficult to avoid optical illusions.

The enormous superiority still distinguishing the smallest security force from the largest multitude did not become clear to me until after the War, because a different law prevails on battlefields inhabited solely by uniformed soldiers. In March of 1921, I witnessed the clash of a three-person machine-gun squad with a demonstration march comprised of as many as 5,000 participants.[31] A minute after the order to fire was given, the demonstrators vanished from the scene even though not one single person had been injured. The sight of this event had something magical about it; it evoked that deep sense of delight which takes hold of one when an ignoble demon is unmasked. At any rate, participation in repelling such an unfounded claim to authority is more instructive than the lessons learned from an entire library of sociological studies. I had a similar impression when, completing street sketches, I made my way in the winter of 1932 to Bülow Square in Berlin, which was the scene of larger political clashes. The clash of an

31. Jünger here describes his experience at Waterloo Square in Hanover, where he was in charge of defending an army base against a large demonstration reacting to the Kapp Putsch of March 1921. As the demonstrators broke through the guarded perimeter of the base, Jünger gave the order to a machine-gun squad to fire a round into the air. The response was a panic in the crowd, and the police were then able to easily restore order. For a detailed account of Jünger's reported experience, see Schwilk, *Ernst Jünger*, pp. 221–22.

organic construction, in which technology and worker-type are unified in purpose, with the masses became particularly visible at Alexander Square as an armored police wagon cut right through a sea of people gripped by a furious rage. It drove straight through the opposing sides. In the face of this armored wagon, the masses found themselves in a purely moral position. They booed and jeered.

On the same day, I also had the opportunity to observe along several side streets the lumpenproletariat, which in no way is of the world of abstract ideas, as is the case with the masses. Bakunin was right in regarding the lumpenproletariat as a much more effective revolutionary force.[32] Seen from the other side, one can say it's enough to disperse the masses, while the lumpenproletariat must be sought out in its hiding places. Its greater effectivity furthermore suggests that it owns a real battle plan, the age-old formation of the pack. The lumpenproletariat's relation to pain is also much more substantial, if no doubt negative. The masses kill with machines, they tear apart and trample underfoot; by contrast, the lumpenproletariat is directly familiar with the joys of torture. The masses are moved morally; they unite in situations of excitement and indignation. They must be convinced that the opponent is evil and that they are prosecuting justice against this evil. The lumpenproletariat is beyond moral valuations and thus always and everywhere ready to seize the opportunity, i.e., with every disturbance of the social order, regardless of origin. The lumpenproletariat therefore functions beyond the more limited space of politics; instead, one must regard the lumpenproletariat as a kind of underground army reserve that the social order keeps on alert. The source of the infernal and crippling vapors is concealed here, which are released to

32. Mikhail Alexandrovich Bakunin (1814–1876) was a Russian revolutionary and anarchist of the nineteenth century.

the surface during times of social upheaval; indeed, this marks the depth of such upheavals, the history of which has yet to be written. The brief number of days during which the masses eliminated their opponents fills the cities with clamor, but there follow other, more dangerous situations where silence reigns. Pain now demands payback on its outstanding debt.

It is to be noted parenthetically here that the word "lumpen-proletariat," as the attentive reader will have not failed to notice, belongs to the outdated vocabulary of class struggle. Yet in truth we are dealing here with an elementary force, which is always present and naturally conceals itself behind the mask of established economic thought. Today, this elementary force appears in new forms associated with other such forces active in political movements and military actions. We refer here above all to the appearance of the partisan, who to a great extent has already lost all its social hue. One assigns the partisan missions to be completed below the legal order. He thus surfaces at the rear of invading armies, where the operations for which he is suited involve espionage, sabotage, and subversion. In the case of civil war, the operations left to the partisan also include missions beyond the bounds of law. Accordingly, partisan struggles are especially ruthless. The partisan is not protected by law; if caught, he is treated in a summary manner. While in war he is sent into action without uniform, in civil war his party identification card is taken before entering the fray. The partisan's loyalties always remain uncertain. It is never clear whether he belongs to one side or the other, to espionage or counter-espionage, to the police force or those fighting the police force, or to all at once; or altogether whether he is active on behalf of others or simply taking part in his own criminal racket. This ambiguity is an essential aspect of his mission. One can find this in partisan operations around the world today, even if often without being recognized as such—whether we are dealing with some clash in the outlying neighborhood of a city or with cases in city capitals concerning domestic and foreign affairs. We are never to determine who bears responsibility for such incidents, because the threads are lost in an obscure underworld where the lines separating the opposing sides become blurred. In the repeated attempts to transform the partisan into a hero, we thus see an inability to differentiate properly. The partisan is surely a figure of the elementary but not of the heroic world. His downfall lacks a tragic quality; it transpires in a zone where one indeed maintains a dull, passive relation to pain and its secrets, but where nevertheless one is unable to rise above pain. But let us return to the masses.

Recklessness provides the actions of the masses with a special measure of senselessness. Since the masses know no bounds—indeed, are essentially unbounded in their behavior—they tend to pay no heed to precautionary measures, such as erecting outposts, which are self-evident for every disciplined group. In the brief moments of history where power relations become unstable, the rejoicing of the masses fills the air. These are precisely the moments where any general, such as a Cavaignac, Wrangel, or Gallifet, rubs his hands in glee.[33] The French have long been superior to us in dealing with the masses because they are more accustomed to the world of abstract ideas; nonetheless, they also had to pay a price early on for this lesson. The massacre of the communards could still

33. Louis-Eugène Cavaignac (1802–1857) was a French general who became de facto head of state with dictatorial powers during the June Days Uprising of 1848 in Paris. He was responsible for crushing the insurrection in Paris; Friedrich Heinrich Ernst Count von Wrangel (1784–1877) was a German general who was responsible for the suppression of the riots in Berlin during the Revolution of 1848; Gaston Alexandre Auguste, Marquis de Gallifet (1830–1907) was a French general who played a decisive role in the repression of the Paris Commune of 1871.

be felt up to the end of the World War. As signs of a more robust health now become visible, the idea of the masses disappears altogether in its familiar political-moral sense. On the contrary, those with armed weapons now take delight in a gathering of unarmed individuals. In the despotic regimes of the Renaissance, one occasionally saw in the assembly of parliamentarians the easiest opportunity to give them a sound thrashing, were one not inclined to wait until one of the larger church festivals for such a chance. By the way, the joy with which figures like Burckhardt, Gobineau, and their epigones chronicled such events is not without consequence for history, just as a generation's historical predilections have always been revealing.[34]

Today, as noted, we are in the process of creating new, more disciplined formations, which, as we will soon see, extend far beyond the more limited sphere of politics. Even in parliamentary democracies, as Germany's most recent history has shown, it is evident that the political parties have lost the people's trust with respect to their most significant source of legitimacy, i.e., in the simple number of votes, and have thus sought to evolve into forces of a different kind. Next to the army and the police there were a series of standing military organizations, and it is truly remarkable that life can run its normal course under such circumstances. The case was similar in medieval Florence, where separate guarded castles with towers stood ominously opposed to one another.

Yet everything is interrelated, and the old and the new intersect in multifarious ways. On the one hand, we see new groups

34. Jacob Burckhardt (1818–1897) was a prominent Swiss historian of art and culture, and is perhaps best known for his *The Civilization of the Renaissance in Italy* (1860). Joseph Arthur Comte de Gobineau (1816–1882) was a French novelist and thinker best known for his racial theories, expounded in *An Essay on the Inequality of the Human Races* (1853–55).

forming solely to safeguard basic democratic rights, especially the right to free association and speech. On the other hand, it seems curious today that no one has yet rejected the call-up of immense, amorphous masses of human beings in those states undergoing real historic transformation. Of course, one cannot ignore the important change happening here: the masses have been left with only *one* liberty, the liberty to consent. Parliaments and plebiscites are being transformed ever more clearly into acts of acclamation, whose manufacture replaces the free formation of public opinion. But this manufacture of consent signifies nothing other than the transformation of the masses from a moral agent into an object.

11.

The growing objectification of the individual and its formations seen today is not new. It is rather an essential characteristic of all spaces, where pain belongs to the immediate and self-evident experiences of life and must be regarded as a feature of intense military preparation. The feeling of intimacy, the belief in self-evident, if not symbolic, values essentially vanishes, and in their place groups still full of conviction are governed by immense detachment. The Church of Smyrna's circular concerning the martyrdom of the holy Polykarp explains the calm composure of believers condemned to be thrown to the lions: "The martyrs of Christ thus prove to us all that at the time of their torture they were absent from their flesh." Similar statements are found on almost every page of Cassian's important portrayal of the creation of cloisters and the lives of the settlers in the Syrian and Egyptian deserts.[35] In Flavius Josephus's writings we find the wonderful depiction of a

35. John Cassian (ca. 360–435) was a Christian theologian, Scythian monk, and Desert Father. See "Conference on Abbot Piamun: On the Three Sorts of Monks," in Cassian's *Conferences*.

disinterested observer of the Roman legion's order of march. We see army units, directed like living machines and by invisible commands, penetrate the flatlands, deserts, and mountains. We see how every evening the camp is pitched with a magical skill and how with equal ease it vanishes in the morning without a trace. We see, finally, how the battle takes place at the "speed of thought." Josephus rightly concluded this account in the following way: "what wonder is it that Euphrates on the east, the ocean on the west, the most fertile regions of Libya on the south, and the Danube and the Rhine on the north, are the limits of this empire? One might well say that the Roman possessions are not inferior to the Romans themselves."[36]

We consider it therefore a mark of superior achievement when life gains distance from itself or, in other words, when it is able to sacrifice itself. This is *not* the case wherever life is regarded as the ultimate value rather than as an outpost. If the most historic moments of life are identical with life's objectification, then life's technology, i.e., its discipline, must be at all times extraordinary. We considered briefly the objectification of the individual and its formations, and we take them to be a good sign. This examination would not be complete, however, if it did not touch upon a third and colder order that bestows its unique character on our time of change. The growing objectification of our life appears most distinctly in technology, this great mirror, which is sealed off in a unique way from the grip of pain. *Technology is our uniform.* Yet we are too deeply immersed in this process to comprehend it to its full extent. If one gains even a little distance, for instance when one returns from a trip to regions hardly touched by technology, the claim on life becomes more visible. This is all the more so to the extent that the character of convenience attached to our

36. The quote here is from Flavius Josephus, *The Wars of the Jews or History of the Destruction of Jerusalem*, bk. 3, chap. 5, par. 7.

technology increasingly merges with the instrumental character of power.

12.

The spectacle of battle is immediately instructive, because here this character of power appears in full light. In the writings of Vegetius, Polybius, or other authors dealing with the art of war in antiquity, we gain the impression that the deployment of war machinery lends military clashes a mathematical quality.[37] Especially in Julius Caesar's prose we find preserved the language of a mind that does not possess a pathos of distance[38] but instead the inborn noble detached judgment requisite for sovereign rule. This language is irrefutably like an object, and in a statement like "res ad triarios venit" the cries of those attacking and dying in battle are muted.[39] The field general's higher judgment perceives things in a way unaffected by pain and passion.

If one can regard the legion as a machine, as a mobile barricade of shields and weapons of assault supported on both flanks by horsemen and catapults, then the entire nature of ancient military technology becomes apparent in the assault on the most significant symbol of security, that is, in the assault on the city walls. We possess a wealth of historical accounts portraying in great detail how cities were besieged

37. Publius Flavius Vegetius Renatus was a fourth-century Roman military expert who wrote an influential military treatise, *Epitoma rei militaris* (*The Military Institutions of the Romans*). Polybius (ca. 203–120 BC) was a Greek historian famous for his *The Rise of the Roman Empire*.

38. Jünger's note: "The 'pathos of distance' is not a feature of *power* but of the *will* to power."

39. "Res venit ad triarios" is translated literally as "the matter comes to the triarier," which signified that the third line of soldiers, who were the oldest and most experienced, were being forced into combat by attacking forces. This final line of defense would decide the outcome of a battle.

with tortoise formations, covered battering-rams, scorpions,[40] rolling turrets, and inclined planes. It is as if these fascinating accounts depicted a clash of demons or of fabulous creations from an extinct animal world. In these spectacles of battle, we lose sight of the fact that we are dealing with human beings; the skillful organization and logical facility at work divert the eye from personal fortunes. Man appears more invulnerable when lodged in rolling vehicles, and this did not fail to intimidate those under attack. In the World War the new armored vehicles had success at first because they hit the enemy like surprise attacks. In these tanks we can sense the magical reaction horsemen evoke in peoples unprepared for attack, as most recently with the Mexicans: they are taken for demonic beings.

Titus's siege of Jerusalem contains a measure of mathematics sought in vain in nineteenth-century military history. In contrast to the armies of the Rococo period, with their rigid lines of formation or rectangles marching over the battlefield in painstaking tempo, the World War's battles of *matériel* are an image of infernal anarchy. The logic underlying this image, as we explained in detail in "Fire and Movement," is directly opposed to the logic of constructive space; we recognize this image wherever a maximal deployment of forces has a minimal effect.[41] This is also why Alexander the Great's battle makes a more majestic impression than the battles of Napoleon. A grand vision requires military formations cast in bronze in order to become truly visible.[42]

40. "Scorpion" was the name given to smaller, more portable *ballistae*, or weapons resembling large crossbows, used by the Roman military.

41. Jünger's essay "Feuer und Bewegung oder Kriegerische Mathematik" also appeared in *Blätter und Steine* (1934). This essay was first printed under the title "Kriegerische Mathematik" in 1930, in the journal *Widerstand*, edited by Ernst Niekisch. See Jünger, "Kriegerische Mathematik," *Widerstand: Zeitschrift für nationalrevolutionäre Politik*, vol. 5, no. 9 (1930): 267–73.

42. The reference is to Alexander the Great's Battle of Issus against the Persians in 333 BC.

We have to realize that the elements of such military formations are now definitely present in our environs and technology.
This is important, because our history will be decided by a
mind capable of grasping and shaping these elements. The
underlying goal of our mission is hidden here behind all the
misunderstandings of our times.

The sight of sea battles in particular proves that even in our
times complex military formations are possible. This is not
accidental, since the World War was, despite its name, essentially a continental and colonial war; this fact corresponds to
its outcome, which, when one looks past the slogans, lies in
the conquest of provinces and colonies. But the World War
also contained the rudiments of imperial conquest, which was
correctly regarded to rely on a naval fleet—swimming outposts of immense power, armored vessels in which the claim
to supremacy is concentrated in the smallest of spaces.

A clash of naval ships is distinguished by its unprecedented
clarity. We can recall in our minds the course of naval battles
right down to the minute and individual shells fired. Moreover, one sees neither the sailor, as he is invisible in a way more
significant than purely physical, nor a mass of soldiers; instead,
one sees the naval fleet or ship. We have before us one of those
cases where man accepts his downfall as fate. His ultimate
concern is no longer to try to avoid this fate, but to ensure that
it takes place with a flag held high. In survivors' accounts, one
repeatedly comes across a remarkable attitude that leads one
to believe that in the decisive moments death is simply not
seen. This is especially true wherever in the zone of annihila-
tion man's focus remains squarely on utilizing weaponry. Only
he who feels secure in immediate proximity to death finds
himself in the highest state of security.

In the meantime, technology's inherent claim to power
has grown stronger. The difference and resistance of nature's

four elements recede as this development unfolds. This fact implies, however, that strategic military campaigns can be realized with greater clarity. In the battles of *matériel*, we see how a field general's mind is not able to penetrate the chaotic zone of fire and terrain; his vision is obscured by the mayhem of tactical maneuvers. Nevertheless, we also have indications that precise military maneuvers, which until recently only seemed possible in the more fluid element of water, are now at least imaginable on land and above all in the newly conquered skies. A feature pointing to the development of more rigorous battle formations can also be found in the concept of the squad, which is now beginning to play a significant role far and wide. Moreover, it is revealing to see how the tank, which in the organic as well as mechanical world possesses a secret relation to mathematics, is being resurrected in new forms at all stages of ground warfare.

The increasing mobility of battle operations, which our technological age strives to achieve in the construction of new war machinery, promises not only a renewal of strategic operations but also heralds the rise of a more hardened and invulnerable type of soldier. The new logic broached earlier in connection to the principles of liberal education also impacts the soldier. In a world where warfare assumes the peculiar character of work, we can no longer speak of a people in arms in the traditional sense. Just as technology is superior to every imaginable deployment of human forces, so too do the teams operating this military technology presuppose a selection process different from universal military conscription. The short duration of military service typical for training the masses is no longer adequate to ensure the requisite mastery of weaponry and personal discipline. Only logically, then, we witness today how training now begins at an early age and is becoming specialized in many ways.

A set of growing concerns thus makes it probable that in the future the army will gain a more objective character with respect to weaponry and personnel. This implies greater clarity and purity in issues related to power. The "ultima ratio regis" engraved on the cannons of the World War in truth had meaning only as a tribute to the past. In reality, a war's popularity is the prerequisite for participation of the masses in military service. The decisive factor had its foundation in conceptions of democracy and justice. The so-called war cabinet thus stood in particularly ill repute. Yet it is beyond doubt that anyone analyzing in an unbiased way the essence of power relations will prefer a war cabinet's war over a popular war. The former is a carefully deliberated war, which has specific objectives and whose timing can be chosen based on objective circumstances. Most important, however, is its remove from the moral zone; it thus has no need to stir up the base instincts and hatreds that the masses require in order to go to war at all.

The decision over war and peace is the highest sovereign prerogative. As such, it presupposes an army capable of being utilized as an instrument of a sovereign will. This relation is imaginable only in a space where there are more important things than pain and where one knows "eternal life" is possible only in the face of death.

13.

Let us now discuss a matter we hold to be self-evident, yet no less noteworthy. Man is most revealing in areas of life where he sees no problems and everything is beyond dispute.

How is it that while debates rage on from all opposing sides about the pros and cons of capital punishment for homicide, we can hardly find a difference of opinion concerning the countless victims of technology, especially those linked to modern forms of transportation? This was not always the case.

A draft of the first law on railroads, for example, clearly cites the goal to make the railroad industry responsible for all damages resulting from its operations. Today, by contrast, people have adopted the opposite opinion. Pedestrians are not only required to conform to traffic laws but are also answerable for infractions against them. This regulation of traffic is a characteristic feature of the technical revolution subjecting man silently and assuredly to the logic of a transformed world.

It never crosses our minds to do without commercial flight, yet its history is full of plane crashes and, viewed simply as a means of transportation, it contradicts all laws of economics. The same mind that lets this fact go unquestioned is also inclined to consider the pain inflicted in monasteries throughout the centuries as a curious folly. Traffic victims are given year in and year out; they've reached a number surpassing the losses resulting from bloody wars. We accept these victims as a foregone conclusion, which reminds us of the life prospects of older professions, such as seamen or miners. In a debate over capital punishment, Bismarck inserted the argument that the thought never occurs to us to stop mining just because we can calculate statistically the number of victims it will claim. He maintained the belief that pain is among the unavoidable facts of the world—an essential conviction of all conservative thinking. In truth, statistics offer further proof that man must pay destiny a high price. It is also noteworthy that suicide rates remain roughly the same regardless of the fortune or misfortune of the times.

The victims claimed by technological processes seem unavoidable, because they conform to our type, i.e., to the worker-type. The worker-type rushes in to fill the empty spaces left behind by the professional trades and conveys to them his peculiar values. A hundred years ago it was normal for a young man to die in a duel; today, such a death would be a curiosity. At around the same time, one considered Berblinger, the Tailor of Ulm, a fool for crashing his airplane contraption into the Danube, and an inexperienced climber breaking his neck on a mountaintop would have been possessed by spleen. Today, on the contrary, death is taken for granted as something to be anticipated while flying a glider or participating in winter sports.

<h2 style="text-align:center">14.</h2>

If one were to characterize with a single word the type of human being taking shape today, one might say that one of its most salient features lies in its possession of a "second" consciousness. This second and colder consciousness reveals itself in the ever-increasing ability to see oneself as an object. This is not to be confused with the act of self-reflection associated with traditional psychology. Psychology differs from the second consciousness. Psychology takes the sensitive human being as its object of inquiry, whereas the second consciousness is focused on the person standing outside the zone of pain. Here, of course, there are still points of overlap. As one is bound to witness in every process of disintegration, psychology too has a rigorous side. This can be seen especially in those branches where psychology has evolved into a pure system of measurement.

Far more revealing, however, are the symbols that the second consciousness seeks to produce. We are not only the first living creatures to work with artificial limbs; through the use of artificial sense organs, we also find ourselves in the process of erecting unusual realms with a high degree of accord between man and machine. This is closely connected with the objectification of our view of life and thus also with our relation to pain.

A first case in point is the revolutionary fact of photography. Images recorded in photographs are accorded documentary status. The World War was the first great event recorded in this way, and since then there is no important event that the artificial eye fails to capture. The aim is to expose spaces otherwise inaccessible to the human eye. The artificial eye penetrates fog banks, haze, and darkness, even the resistance of matter itself. Telescopes are set to work in the depths of oceans and at great heights in observation balloons.

The photograph stands outside of the zone of sensitivity. It has a telescopic quality; one can tell that the event photographed is seen by an insensitive and invulnerable eye. It records the bullet in mid-flight just as easily as it captures a man at the moment an explosion tears him apart.[43] This is our own peculiar way of seeing, and photography is nothing other than an instrument of our own peculiar nature. Remarkable that this peculiarity is still hardly visible in other areas, such as literature; but if we can expect something more from literature as well as painting, the description of the most minute psychic processes will no doubt be replaced by a new kind of precise, objective depiction.

We already pointed out in *The Worker* that photography is a weapon of the worker-type. For him, seeing is an act of assault. Correspondingly, the endeavor to make oneself invisible grows, as is already seen in the use of "camouflage" during the World War. A military position could no longer be held once detected by aerial reconnaissance. These circumstances lead constantly toward a greater plasticity and objectivity. Today we find rifles mounted with scopes, and even torpedoes for air and sea made with optical guidance.

43. In 1931, Jünger wrote an introduction, entitled "Über die Gefahr," for a collection of essays and images of such moments of imminent death (Ferdinand Buchholtz, ed., *Der gefährliche Augenblick* [Berlin: Junker und Dunnhaupt Verlag, 1931]). An English version of Jünger's essay can be found under the title "On Danger," in *New German Critique*, vol. 59 (Spring/Summer 1993): 27–32.

In politics, too, the photograph is among those weapons used with ever greater mastery. Photography, in particular, seems to offer the worker-type a means to hunt down the individual as an opponent no longer capable of defending his ways—the private sphere is no match for photography. It is also easier to change one's attitude than one's face. The practice of placing photographs of people murdered in political clashes on posters is of immense maliciousness.

Photography, then, is an expression of our peculiarly cruel way of seeing. Ultimately, it is a kind of evil eye, a type of magical possession. One senses this very clearly in places where a different cultic substance is still active. The moment a city like Mecca can be photographed, it falls into the colonial sphere.

We have a peculiar and almost indescribable urge to endow processes of life with the character of a microscopic slide. Today, important events are engulfed by photographic lenses and microphones and lit up by bursts of flashing cameras. Often the event itself is completely subordinate to its "broadcast"; it thereby turns to a great degree into an object. We have grown accustomed to political trials, parliamentary meetings, and contests whose real purpose is to be the object of international broadcast. The event is bound neither to a particular space nor to a particular time, because it can be shown anywhere and as often as one likes. These are the signs of an immense detachment, and the question arises whether this second consciousness we now see so tirelessly at work will be given a core set of values able to provide a deeper justification to the growing petrification of life.

This detachment is even clearer in the transmission of images—through broadcast of photographs in a second space less accessible to sensitivity. This is most evident where we confront our own reflection, whether by watching our movements on film or hearing our voice as if it belonged to a stranger.

The amount of pain we can endure increases with the progressive objectification of life. It almost seems as if man seeks to create a space where pain can be regarded as an illusion, but in a radically new way. It would be worthwhile, then, to more closely analyze films, which lend Tertullian's writing on the Roman Games fresh relevance.[44] It is astonishing that grotesque films made up of a handful of painful and horrifying accidents arouse wild laughter. Filming as a technical process, which records and interrupts human action, evokes a revealing bias for mathematical formulas. Certain actions are especially suited for film, such as a skier taking a precise run down an icy slope. The realm of masks, marionettes, puppets, and mannequins also belongs here—a realm in which artificial creatures move themselves through the sound of mechanically produced voices. We are also struck by the synchronicity of events, where images of luxurious comfort are interrupted by photos of a catastrophe simultaneously wreaking havoc on the other end of the globe. The spectator's involvement is conspicuously silent. This silence is more abstract and crueler than the wild rage one can witness in the southern arenas, where in the bullfight, for instance, remnants of the Ancient Games are still preserved.

Here is the occasion to note that while watching a bullfight, which springs from an ancient cult of the earth, the logic of the ritual masks the actual feeling of pain. We are forced to make the same observation wherever a bloody encounter, such as a students' duel, happens in accord with the rules of chivalry. In the world of the worker, ritual is replaced by a precise

44. Quintus Septimius Florens Tertullianus or Tertullian (ca. 160–235) was a church leader and prolific author of Early Christendom. See Tertullian's description of the gladiator events in *Apology*, in *The Ante-Nicene Fathers,* ed. Allan Menzies, trans. Rev. S. Thelwall (Grand Rapids, MI: Wm. B. Eerdmanns Publishing Co., 1885), vol. 3, bk. 1, chaps. 9, 15.

technical process, which lacks as much in morality as it does in chivalry. Yet the ethos of these processes—and the very fact that pain can be endured to a higher degree points to such an ethos—remains unknown to the present day.

The secret design of artificial sense organs reveals spaces in which catastrophe plays a central role. In such spaces, the dispatch of commands must be more dependable, systematic, and secure. We are approaching the point where a news report, public warning, or imminent threat needs to reach us within minutes. Special forms of discipline are hidden behind the entertaining aspect of communications technologies, such as radio and film. With all likelihood, the broader public will become more aware of this, as listening, especially to public radio, becomes an obligation.

15.

In all these events we are dealing less with technical changes than with a new way of life. This is seen most clearly in the fact that the instrumental character of these changes is not restricted to the zone of technology but strives to place the human body under its command.

This is at any rate the meaning of the peculiar activity we call sports. Sports should be distinguished from ancient contests just as much as today's Olympics are from those of the Ancient Greeks. Sports are much less about competition than exact measurement. Neither opponent nor spectator must be present. Instead, the presence of a second consciousness is decisive, which records the event with a tape measure, a stopwatch, electricity, or a photographic lens. It thus becomes irrelevant whether a race, javelin throw, or high jump takes place on tracks next to one another or as far apart as Rhodes and Australia.

The strange desire to document a record down to the smallest spatial and temporal numerical unit comes from a need to know precisely what the human body, as an instrument, is capable of achieving. We can question the meaning of such events, but we cannot deny their existence. They become absurd the moment one no longer grasps them in their symbolic context.

In watching ski jumpers head down the ski ramp one after the other or race drivers flying by like arrows with helmets and uniforms, the impression one has hardly differs from seeing a specially built machine. These connections are also expressed in human habit. Sports in our sense are not that old, and yet the photographs of the first teams with their beards and civil attire already seem odd to us. The new face, as witnessed today in the illustrated magazines, looks different; it is soulless, as if made of metal or hewn out of special timber, and it no doubt has a real relation to photography. It is one of the faces in which the worker-type or race of the worker is expressed. Sports are a part of the work process, which appears especially clearly here because of its lack of real utility. Incidentally, based on this observation one can see readily how normal amateur competition is rooted in old values of honor. Amateur competition is linked above all to those realms preserving a remnant of courtly tradition, such as horse racing and tennis. The exercise of sports, however, is no doubt a real profession.

In analyzing these figures, one cannot avoid, purely based on appearance, the impression that they are far removed from the zone of sensitivity. The human will disciplines and outfits this flesh with such painstaking care that it now seems more indifferent to injury. Today, we again are able to bear the sight of death with greater indifference, since we no longer feel at home in our body as we did before. It no longer accords with our style to stop a flying show or a car race simply because of a deadly accident. Such accidents lie not outside but inside the zone of a new kind of security.

Sports make up only one of the areas where we can observe the hardening, honing, or even galvanizing of the human physique. The desire to see physical beauty in keeping with different standards is no less noteworthy. A close connection to photography is also present here, especially to film, which is essentially the model of beauty. The eye has many occasions to grow accustomed to viewing the naked body, such as in sports, public baths, rhythmic dancing, but also in advertisements. We are dealing here with forays into the erotic zone, whose meaning has yet to be revealed even if we already have an inkling of it.

The ambiguity of such events in an age of transition is especially revealing. It finds expression in the fact that a necessary change appears at first as a new kind of freedom. It is surprising to see, then, that an area of the most sophisticated individualistic pleasure and self-enjoyment like psychology suddenly starts to produce precise systems of measurement. The psycho-technical method constitutes ever more clearly a means to calibrate the demands placed on the race or, what is the same, the worker-type. Notions such as that of reaction time, first developed in an effort to reduce[45] car accidents, convey an image of the objective nature of these demands.

Finally we should mention the extent to which the body has also become an object in the field of medicine. The ambiguity just noted is also evident in this context. On the one hand, narcosis appears as a liberation from pain; on the other hand, it turns the body into an object capable of being treated as if it were lifeless matter. Among the trivial observations one can make in our cities is the novel penchant for drugs with anatomical effects; one registers, for instance, how a sleeping pill

45. Jünger's note: "By the way, formulations such as the 'reconstruction of facts' indicate an altered view of guilt, which to a great extent is devoid of moral connotations."

influences the layers in the cross-section of a brain. Exhibits of this kind were taboo only a few years ago.

16.

We have now assembled sufficient data to conclude that our relation to pain has indeed changed. The spirit that has emerged among us over the past century is indubitably cruel. It leaves its trace on the human condition; it dispenses with the soft spots and hardens the points of resistance. We find ourselves in a situation where we are still capable of grasping what is lost; we can still sense the destruction of values and how the world is becoming more shallow and superficial. New generations are growing up far removed from all our inherited traditions, and it is an amazing feeling to see these children, many of whom will live to experience the year 2000. By then, the last remnants of the modern, i.e., Copernican, age will most likely have disappeared.

In the meantime, the historic state of affairs is clearly upon us. Of course, it was already grasped by every true mind of the nineteenth century, and each of these figures, from Hölderlin onward and far beyond Europe's borders, has left behind an esoteric teaching on pain—because here is hidden the true testing ground of reality.

Today, we see the valleys and plains full of armies, military deployments, and exercises. We see states more hostile and ready for war than ever before, looking everywhere to expand their power and marshalling military forces and arsenals of weaponry, and their essential aim is no longer in doubt. We also see the individual ever more clearly fall into a state where he can be sacrificed without a second thought. The question thus arises whether we are witnessing the opening act of the spectacle to come, in which life appears as the will to power, and nothing else?

We saw that man is able to resist the assault of pain to the degree that he is capable of self-detachment. This self-detachment, this functionalization and objectification of life increases uninterruptedly. The age of security has been superseded with surprising speed by another, in which the values of technology prevail. The logic and mathematics now governing life are extraordinary and awe inspiring. One has the feeling the game is too sophisticated and logical for the human mind to have devised.

Yet all this in no way relieves us of responsibility. If one looks at the individual in his lonely state, driven out into dangerous spaces and on high alert, the question concerning the reason for this state of emergency arises. *The* power must be enormous that is capable of subjecting man to demands one places on a machine. Nonetheless, the eye will search in vain for secure spaces above the fray, beyond all uncertainty or doubt, and removed from the processes now preparing for military conflict. But the only things beyond doubt are the destruction of old cults, the impotency of culture, and the wretched mediocrity of the actors.

We conclude, then, that we find ourselves in a last and indeed quite remarkable phase of nihilism, characterized by the broad expansion of new social orders with corresponding values yet to be seen. Once one has grasped the uniqueness of this situation, the seemingly contradictory view of man disappears. One grasps how an enormous organizational capacity can exist alongside a complete blindness vis-à-vis values, belief without meaning, discipline without legitimacy—in short, the surrogate nature of ideas, institutions, and individuals altogether. One grasps why one yearns to see the state in such an instrumental age not as the most universal instrument but as a cultic entity, and why technology and ethos have become synonymous in such a peculiar way.

These are all indications that one has already completely pierced *the* side of the process rooted in obedience, training, and discipline; in short, the side of the human will. And never before have more advantageous circumstances existed for an incantation, superior to the purely moral will, to lend meaning to the not inappreciable virtue of ants. Man's relation to prophecy reveals that in his innermost being he is aware of the situation. For him, the *status quo* in all the states is just the basis for, or transition to, a future social order.

In such a situation, pain remains the only measure promising a certainty of insights. Wherever values can no longer hold their ground, the movement toward pain endures as an astonishing sign of the times; it betrays the negative mark of a metaphysical structure.

The practical consequence of this observation for the individual is, despite everything, the necessity to commit oneself to the preparation for war—regardless of whether he sees in it the preparatory stage of ruin or believes he sees on the hills covered with weather-worn crosses and wasted palaces the storm preceding the establishment of new orders of command.

Also from Telos Press

The Forest Passage
Ernst Jünger

The Adventurous Heart: Figures and Capriccios
Ernst Jünger

Hamlet or Hecuba:
The Intrusion of the Time into the Play
Carl Schmitt

Theory of the Partisan
Carl Schmitt

The Nomos *of the Earth*
in the International Law of the Jus Publicum Europaeum
Carl Schmitt

The Non-Philosophy Project:
Essays by François Laruelle
Gabriel Alkon and Boris Gunjevic, eds.

The Democratic Contradictions of Multiculturalism
Jens-Martin Eriksen and Frederik Stjernfelt

A Journal of No Illusions:
Telos, *Paul Piccone, and the Americanization of Critical Theory*
Timothy W. Luke and Ben Agger, eds.

Class Cleansing: The Massacre at Katyn
Victor Zaslavsky

Confronting the Crisis: Writings of Paul Piccone
Paul Piccone